WAVE CREST

THE GLASS OF C.F. MONROE

Wilfred R. Cohen

COLLECTOR BOOKS

A Division of Schroeder Publishing Co., Inc.

Robert Rameriz photographed the Cohen (all non-attributed photos) and Newland collections. All others were photographed by the author.

Additional copies of this book may be ordered from:

Collector Books
P.O. Box 3009
Paducah, KY 42001

@$29.95 Add $1.00 for postage and handling.

Copyright: Wilfred R. Cohen, 1987

This book or any part thereof may not be reproduced without the written consent of the Author and Publisher.

Printed in Hong Kong by Everbest Printing Co. Ltd. for Four Colour Imports, Ltd., Louisville, Kentucky.

Acknowledgments

Lionel and Arlene De Ragon, West Hartford, CT.
Without their help, this would be a picture book. I met them originally through my interest in biscuit jars, but fortunately for all of us, they are interested in research and geneology. I am indebted to them for almost all the information on the background of the company and C.F. Monroe, himself.

R. Shawn Bradway.
Probably the earliest and finest dealer in C.F. Monroe glass and other opal ware, I am indebted to him for allowing me to use his pamphlet on the company. He has been out of business for almost ten years, much to the loss of all of us.

Elsa Grimmer, Winfield, IA.
Elsa published the first book on Wave Crest and reproduced the first known catalogue, a major step forward for collectors. Her unselfish encouragement and especially her friendship are greatly valued.

Tom Neale and Glen Schlotfeldt, Bridgewater, VA.
One can only use superlatives in talking about these two dealers-collectors. No one works harder, tries harder, and remembers better than these two. They are always willing and ready to help, and indeed have helped other authors. They are fine people and loyal friends.

Whitney and Charlene Newland, Santa Barbara, CA.
Carrol and Don Lyle, Tacoma, WA.
Richard and Mary McGaw, IL.
Gerry Andes, Kingsport, TN.
Hubert Gillian, Kingsport, TN.
Dee's Antiques, Meriden, CT.
A thousand thanks to the above, all collectors, who allowed me to enter their very private homes and turn them inside out so that we all might be richer for it. No one person can possibly see, own, or find everything, and they all helped in making this book as comprehensive as possible.

Douglas and Margaret Archer, Kermersville, NC.
Thanks to long time friends, authors, collectors, and now shop owners, for their interest.

Meriden Historical Society, Meriden, CT.
Thanks for their help in finding some background for this book.

Corning Museum of Glass, Corning, NY.
My appreciation for the supplement of the 1900-1901 catalogue from their archives.

My wife, Dolli, for her help, encouragement, & tolerance.

My daughter, Carol, for her typing.

Foreword

It is amazing to me how little is known about the C.F. Monroe Company. I have tried to find out what I could, but precious little seems to exist. I wanted to present a background on the company as well as a pictorial of the glass. However, our forebears, eighty to ninety years ago, did not consider the collector of today. I have been told that when C.F. Monroe went out of business in 1916, everything was literally tossed out of the factory into dumps and abandoned wells. This must be true, because I have been unable to uncover any advertising material about the company other than what is reproduced here from the *Meriden Daily Journal*. Nothing whatsoever is extant, at this writing, on Nakara or Kelva. After thirteen years of searching, I have found original Wave crest catalogues for 1895-1896 and for 1899-1900. Unfortunately, there is nothing in the latter that is not in the former, or the catalogue of 1900-1901 already reprinted by Elsa Grimmer. Perhaps this book will be a stimulant for some hidden (written) treasures to be unearthed.

The following ad appeared in the Newtown Bee, a well-read antiques newspaper in Connecticut, and did not draw one single response!

The author encourages readers to contact him with any additional information that comes to light, whether it be pictures of unusual pieces, advertisements, catalogues, newspaper clippings, etc. Corrections of wrong or inaccurate material in this book would be especially appreciated. If enough new material is uncovered, an updated version or addendum could be added.

Also, I wonder if there is enough interest to start a C.F. Monroe Club similar to other collector's clubs.

All letters will be answered. A self-addressed, stamped envelope (SASE) is appreciated and will facilitate a prompt reply.

Wilfred R. Cohen
P.O. Box 27151
Santa Ana, CA 92799

Charles Fabian Monroe:

His Days Before Wave Crest

In 1877, it appears that Charles F. Monroe's initial job as a decorator was with The Meriden Flint Glass Company. He was often sent abroad to study and observe new designs and techniques by European glass manufacturers.

The following story, culled from the *Meriden Journal* of Friday, January 14, 1887, recounts an adventure embarked upon by C.F. Monroe in 1876.

CHARLEY MONROE'S CANOE TRIP

THE LONG AND PERILOUS TRIP THAT HE MADE IN IT

Almost lost off Point Judith, but Rescued by a Fisherman - His Big Reception in New York and Philadelphia After His Successful Voyage.

Probably very few people in this city, aside from his intimate friends, have ever heard the story of Charles F. Monroe's adventures on the water in 1876, when he made the famous trip in a cloth covered canoe from New Bedford to Philadelphia, a distance of 430 miles. At that time Mr. Monroe was in the employ of the New England Glass works as a glass decorator, and while there on the shores of Buzzard's Bay his spirit of adventure led him to construct several small canoes in which he daily paddled down Buzzard's Bay in the teeth of the hardest gales that blew in from the ocean. His companions laughed at the seaworthiness of his craft, and then to decide a wager, Mr. Monroe determined to build a canoe in which he would make the voyage from New Bedford to Philadelphia to the Centennial.

He built a frame-work and covered it with painted canvas. When he finished he had a canoe fourteen feet, six inches long and twenty-three inches wide, with a water tight compartment at each end. The M. Eugenie, as he called it, was visited by thousands of people who scoffed as did all the papers at the possibility of his ever completing the trip. Nevertheless on

August 7, Mr. Monroe made a start. Excursion steamers followed him down the bay and saw the start, which was depicted in all the illustrated papers at that time. The rest of the story is best told in Mr. Monroe's own words:

" I had been accustomed" said he, "to go out in my little craft in the very worst of weather and was certain that I could go through to the end of the trip provided I could hold out physically to the end. I was then twenty years old and weighed 127 pounds, but was muscular for my weight. The entire strain comes in the muscles of the chest and arms, and you can imagine the immense strain that 430 miles of paddling, many of them against a head tide, I was subject to. My friends and the papers tried to discourage me but I started off on August 7 with heavy sea and made directly for Newport. I reached Westport that night and got a good night's rest. The next morning early I started for Newport. Off Cuttyhunk the seas were running mountains high and the sun poured down on my head, but I finally reached Newport Harbor. The news of my voyage preceded me and all along the shore wherever I touched, crowds of people came down to the shore to see the curosity. On the following morning I started from Newport before daylight for Narragansett Pier where I took breakfast. I knew the hardest work of the trip was before me in rounding Point Judith, the roughest spot on the whole coast where I was out on the ocean. I paddled down toward the point and had struck the roughest spot. The sun was beating on my head with not a breath of wind stirring and a heavy swell rolling from the sea. The two previous days told on me and overcame me. I tried to rise but could not for a long time. When I finally came to myself a fisherman was gazing at me. He tried to dissuade me, but I went on in the morning to Charleston Point and was taken care of by a party of bathers. The same afternoon I started for Watch Hill, which I could see in the distance. I arrived after dark at the lifesaving station and was taken at once to the Larkins House and seated with a lot of ladies. Imagine my condition! The sleeves of my shirt had shrunk from the wrist to the elbows and my hands and arms and face were blistered from exposure to the sun. Then I went to bed and started the next morning for New London. Head tides kept me back and I only reached Stonington. Those days are samples of my sufferings.

One eye was entirely closed and the other ran. Where the blisters had peeled off, my arms were raw and bleeding and the salt water hardly made them feel better, but I kept straight on until at last I reached New York. There I stayed three days, the guest of various clubs and organizations for I was the pioneer of canoeing and my trip was the subject for long column articles on my progress each day. After my rest there I made my start for Philadelphia. Up the Raritan canal my adventures were many but at last I reached Philadelphia, the biggest curiosity of the whole centennial. For four days the receptions, etc., that were tendered me kept the excitement up, and then reaction setting in, I took to my bed, and for two weeks lay in a fever. But I accomplished my ends and would like to do it again."

Mr. Monroe has a large scrap book filled with clippings from many of the papers of that time, with startling headlines and illustrations of some of the perils he passed through on his voyage. He returned to New Bedford, and there he helped to found the New Bedford Yacht Club, one of the most flourishing organizations along the coast.

Having read this article perhaps gives us a little insight into the character of C.F. Monroe, the man.

Since there is nothing available by way of a biography we must piece together what we can from news in the local papers.

In the year 1880, Charles Monroe opened his first shop, offering to the public imported glassware. This shop apparently flourished and before long we find notice of the opening of a glass decorating studio and elegant show rooms for the display of art and glass objects. On Wednesday, September 13, 1882 we find the following column published in the *Meriden Daily Republican*:

Charles F. Monroe has completed the furnishing of his new decorative art rooms in Guy's building on West Main Street, and today opened the doors to the public for inspection. His parlors are on the west side of the building, and are large and spacious. Besides his art business, the rooms are devoted to the showing of the Meriden Flint Glass Company's ware. An elegant Brussels carpet is on the floor, its unique pattern and handsome trimmings making it very noticeable. Over the windows, and over the arch door to the decorating rooms are draped heavy damask curtains giving the room a rich and luxuriant appearance. In the center of the room is one of Bradley & Hubbard's eight-light brass chandeliers, which when lighted makes the room as bright as day. A large black walnut table in the center of the room is devoted to various works of art, both in the statuette and decorative line. A new and comparitively cheap line of plaster medalions, from works of the old masters, is very prominent on the center of the table. It's particular beauty and value is the manner in which the most minute features and characteristics of art are preserved. Paintings from the brush of F. Miller, the Boston artist, whose work is day by day growing more popular with the lovers of expensive paintings, are predominant. His strong forte in painting is in animals; the most noticeable being a brood of chickens deliberating over the mastication of a bumble bee. A couple of rabbits and a brace of partridges would lead a person to believe that they were looking at the game in reality as they hung upon the wall. A fox, Mr. Miller's materpiece, painted from an animal he raised for the purpose of painting it in various positions, is one of the most noticeable of all. Mr. Monroe has shown a great deal of enterprise in giving the appreciative people of Meriden a chance to furnish themselves with the finest work without being obliged to go to New York or Boston for them, and it is hoped he has not thrown his time and money away, but will be aided to further the advancement of art in this city. A full line of cut glass in two large and elegant black walnut cases give the parlors the most finished and complete look imaginable. Mr. Monroe would be pleased to show all who care to call, the many rare and beautiful pieces of work that we have not room to describe.

The *Meriden Daily Republican* had a column on Fridays each week which was along the lines of a public interest review, mentioning such items as parties, engagements, plays and business about town. On the 5th of January 1883, there are two items regarding C.F. Monroe, as follows:

Business is good at the Meriden Flint Glass Co., and to keep up with their orders they are obliged to run full time. The platers and buffers will begin work in the Britannia shop on Monday. The remainder of the factory will start up on the 15th.

A seven foot decorated mirror at Monroe's Art Room on Main Street, is the cause of much comment by the lovers of decorative art in this city.

On page 287, headed "Review of the State of Connecticut" in the 1883 *Connecticut Historical and*

Industrial Magazine there is a sub-heading "C.F. Monroe" which reads as follows:

Art Rooms, No. 36 West Main Street .-The only art parlors in the city are those of Mr. C.F. Monroe, in the handsome private house at 36 West Main Street. Mr. Monroe is a Rhode Island man, a practical artist, and one of the best decorators in the country, as well as an experienced teacher of glass and china decorating. He has had excellent and practical opportunities for studying his art, having visited the principal art galleries in Europe, also different potteries, china and glass factories, and has been connected as designer and decorator with a number of Eastern Manufacturers. He is the decorator for the Meriden Flint Glass Co., and is also connected with the large house of Bradley & Hubbard, to the extent of exhibiting samples of, and taking orders for, their handsome bronzes and other wares. He has his studio in the rear of his art parlors, where he decorates tiles to order for household use, lamp shades, porcelain, etc. He aims to make his rooms the art centre of Meriden, and thus help to educate the people in art matters. He keeps in stock a fine assortment of bric-a-brac, specimens of the beautiful cut glass of the Meriden Flint Glass Co., a complete line of artists' materials, the Rogers and Florentine Statuary, and a permanent exhibition of oil paintings by American artists chiefly, from which the art-loving citizens of the town can select pictures for their homes. His first annual art exhibition was held in the spring of 1883, and the catalogue contained eighty works, by such well-known artists as Geo. H. and James D. Smillie, J.H. Dolph, Wm. Gedney Bunce, A.F. Bellows, J.F. Cropsey, H. Bolton Jones, R.M. Shurtliff, Arthur Parton, Krusemand, Van Elton, J.B. Bristol, H.H. Wyant, M.F. H. De Hass and C.H. Gifford and many other well-known metropolitan artists. Mr. Monroe pays great attention to holiday goods, and it is his intention to exchange frequently with art stores in Boston and New York, giving the citizens of Meriden a choice collection from which to select.

Searching through copies of the *Meriden Daily Republic* again, we find some rather sad news on the 4th of March in 1885. It is a brief note, but reproves the citizens for their lack of appreciation of the finer things:

The Art Room To Be Closed

Meriden art lovers will be sorry to learn that C.F. Monroe is to give up the art store, although he is to continue to occupy the same apartments, devoting them to his new Art academy and the sale of artists' materials. It is a pity that Meriden, a city of over 20,000 inhabitants, can not support one first class art store! All his stock, excepting artists' materials, is being sold for less than cost. Already some of the fine engravings and paintings have found ready purchasers, and a great many elegant goods can be bought at a great sacrifice. It is to be hoped that the art school will prove such a success that Mr. Monroe will feel encouraged enough to open his store again.

This may be the reason that in 1885 it was noted that he was the manager of the Meriden Roller Rink Company, possibly a job between his decorating studios.

Almost a month prior to the above news item being published, it was announced in the same newspaper that Mr. Monroe was about to open his Art Academy. The announcement told of classes planned for three days a week and the need to enroll at least 100 students. The Academy was to be an experiment and indeed C.F. Monroe made it known that he would not continue it for more than a week if it did not prove to be a success immediately. Apparently his efforts at making the endeavor profitable were a success because in the course of six months the Art Room and Academy upstairs were thriving. Another report on August 29th stated that the cultural growth in the city was due in great part to C.F. Monroe's efforts to educate the populace of Meriden in the appreciation of fine art works."

We read again in the *Daily Republican* of August 29 that encouraging progress has been enjoyed by the Art Academy.

ART IN MERIDEN

Progress Made During The Past Year

It is pleasant to note the advance made here in matters pertaining to art during the past twelve months. The secret of the increased interest is the fact that Meriden's business men have taken hold of the subject. Always first in any enterprise that tends towards the city's growth and prosperity, they have shown an earnest desire to promote a taste for that which cannot result but in the refinement and cultivation of the people. Art is one of the higher grades of education, and one reason why Meriden has been backward in this branch, is that the people have had little chance to study it, until Mr. Monroe opened his art rooms here.

Mr. Monroe said to-day that he has every reason to feel satisfied with the progress that

has been made in the art line, and believes his efforts to provide a place where this fascinating study can be pursued have been fully appreciated. The tendency here has not been in favor of cheap goods, but for a high class of work. Meriden people are not to be put off with indifferent articles, which are bought because of their cheapness. The ladies here are learning to paint and are studying art, and are becoming critical judges.

The purchases of fine oil paintings have been encouraging. Since he opened his rooms, about a year ago, Mr. Monroe had sold 25 costly works. Meriden should congratulate itself on having one of the cosiest little art rooms in New England. The latest purchase is Albert Insley's "On the Hackensack" by Mr. N.L. Bradley.

As the year 1885 progresses, we have found small notices of good things happening, and this brings us up through May of 1886.

September 24, 1885 - C.F. Monroe is making extensive preparation for an exhibit at the Danbury Fair.

October 14, 1885 - C.F. Monroe has received an order to paint on a tile a picture of the old homestead of Mrs. E.P. Weed of Norwalk. The panel which will be an elegant piece of work will be placed in that lady's handsome residence in Norwalk, Connecticut.

1886 - M.D.R. Saturday, May 22, 1886. C.F. Monroe will move into his new quarters in the Carter Bldg., State Street; the middle of next week, where his facilities will be ample to meet requirements of his constantly increasing business.

The following is the wording in a small advertisement from "Meriden and Vicinity" Business Directory of May 1886:

ART DECORATORS--GLASS
C.F. MONROE,
49 State Street, Meriden, Conn., opal glass decorating works. Hand decorated work to match rooms in color and design, on glass shades, lamps, vases, plaques, tiles for mantles and paneling. Table salt spills, in large variety at low price.

From the *Meriden Daily Journal* of Saturday, May 12, 1886, we find news of some exciting expansions of the business of C.F. Monroe.

ANOTHER NEW FACTORY

C.F. Monroe to Build One
on Capital Avenue.

C.F. Monroe has bought the lot west of the Meriden & Waterbury railroad track on Capital avenue and will build a factory there, in which to carry on his increasing decorating business. The land was bought from Asaph Merriam. It is 145 feet on the railroad side, 124 feet on Capitol avenue, and 157 feet deep.

The shop will be seventy-five feet long, thirty-five feet wide and two and a half stories high. Mr. Monroe will put in four new kilns in addition to those now in use at his present shop and employ seventy-five new hands.

When finished the new shop will be one of the most complete decorating establishments in the country. It will cost about $6,000. H.C. Wilcox has interested himself in having Mr. Monroe build at the West end and thinks two or three more shops will be built over that way in a few years. Mr. Monroe will break ground next week for the new factory.

June 27, 1890 - The following article obviously refers to the new establishment which was a small landmark on the road into town. (MDJ):

PROVING A GREAT SUCCESS.

[Southington Phoenix.]

The opal glass business of Mr. Monroe, which many Southington people have noticed near the Meriden, Waterbury & Connecticut River railroad, when driving into Meriden, is proving a great success. It will pay anyone to visit the establishment and see the many beautiful things made of glass. A new invention is a lamp shade with silk curtains which promises to be a great success.

1892, Incorporation of the C.F. Monroe Company

The year 1892 marked the formal incorporation of the C.F. Monroe Company. It was then that they began the production of their famous Wave Crest line. It was patented on October 4, 1892. The registration of the Kelva trademark occured in 1904 but NAKARA was never registered for a trademark.

In 1895 the *Meriden Daily Journal*, Souvenir edition reports on a thriving enterprise.

THE C.F. MONROE COMPANY

Another industry which has spread the fame of Meriden to every State in the Union and nearly every Canadian province is that of the C.F. Monroe Company. This company's product figures very largely among those of the largest manufacturing concerns of the city, the company manufacturing innumerable beautiful fancy articles in glass and porcelain, unique in design, suitable for holiday and wedding gifts.

The company gives employment to a large number of artists, all of whom are of the highest skill, and consequently of a superior order of intelligence. In design the company's products show originality and novelty. In fancy articles of porcelain or glass, with gold and silver trimming, this company leads the trade in this country. The wares have justly met the favor of the trade wherever they are shown, and the industry is constantly increasing in magnitude through the vigilant management of its enterprising head.

The buildings are conveniently located alongside the tracks of the Meriden branch of the New England railroad, affording excellent facilities for the shipment of the bulky packages. During the past three years the rapid increase in business has necessitated the addition of a three-story building. Their showroom is one of the chief attractions of Meriden.

The company's capital is $40,000, the stock being held by local capitalists. The officers are: C.F. Monroe, president and treasurer; E.B. Everitt, secretary; W.H. Lyon, H. Wales Lines and Edward Miller, directors.

In order to have an outlet for their goods in a large metropolitan area, the C.F. Monroe Company had established a store and offices in New York, at 42 Murray Street. In 1899 the store and offices were moved to 28 Barclay Street.

It is assumed from both the 1895 and 1900 catalogues that C.F. Monroe sold only to the trade; they did not run a retail store of any sort.

The following article is copied from the "China Glass and Brass Journal" of 1897 and is a marvelous description of the New York sales office:

THE CHINA, GLASS & BRASS JOURNAL 1897

Our illustration represents one of the latest novelties produced by the C.F. Monroe Co., an announcement appears elsewhere. It is a photo holder, the body of opal, richly decorated in tints and designs, and mounted with gold trimmings. A visit to their New York sales office is a revelation to many buyers. They show a beautiful line of goods in what is probably one of the most artistically conceived showrooms in New York.

Elaborately carved partitions divide the whole on either side, the light woodwork being well done by artistic hangings. A large palm in the office reaches to the ceiling and invites rest upon the cushioned centre seat beneath its branches. It and accessories give the buyer an idea and appearance of the wares when displayed in a fine retail store. In the cases, electrically lighted and artistically displayed, are the company's production and partitions are paneled off in plate glass, richly decorated at the C.F. Monroe Co.'s factory. This is to show the class of work the company's decorators are capable of doing. Among the wares shown are jewel and handkerchief boxes, photograph receivers, puff boxes, cigar sets, ash receivers, paper weights, and hundreds of little novelties intended for the wedding and holiday trade. The bodies of these goods are opal, richly hand-decorated in colors, and trimmings are particularly ornate and goldplated items are lined with fine satins in all the art shades. There is also a line of globes and shades.

(Thanks to Bill Heacock for this article.)

In 1902 C.F. Monroe, among others, was appointed to a committee to form plans for enlarged quarters for the Meriden Home Club, the leading social organization of the city. It's active membership was limited to 250 and included the leading business and professional men in the city, while its non-resident membership list was composed of men representative of the best interests of the state. He was further appointed to a special committee of seven, to further plan and obtain subscriptions to the

capital stock to purchase the site, adopt plans and build the club house. This was all done and formally opened in January 1, 1903!

1903 is the date given by all the early references for the start-up of C.F. Monroe's glass cutting dept. A three-story building was constructed at an angle to the main building for glass cutting and over 200 artisans were employed, including experienced glass cutters, apprentices, and designers. Some of the best cut glass in the area came from C.F. Monroe, in an industry that was started in Meriden in the 1800's. At one time Meriden was considered the center of the cut glass industry, which employed 900 people, and had many fine companies.

On May 13, 1902 Carl V. Helmschmied assigned a copyright to a C.F. Monroe Co. design. This appears to be the only one in cut glass.

An interesting "puzzle" has come to light with the 1900-1901 catalogue supplement. As you will see, there are a number of pages of cut glass offered for sale along with the opal ware. As noted above, 1903 is the date given for the inception of glass cutting. Perhaps the company did limited glass cutting in their previous shop, and only got into it in a big way in 1903 with the construction of the new quarters (see page 214).

Some of C.F. Monroe's employees left and started their own cut glass shops in the later years.

The 1906 copy of *Meriden Centennial Edition* tells us a very full story, as follows:

THE C.F. MONROE COMPANY

A concern which for some years has added much fame to Meriden as a manufacturing center and which within recent years has experienced a most remarkable growth is the C.F. Monroe Company. The business was established by Charles F. Monroe in 1886, and has been carried on by him with remarkable success. The history of the business, therefore, for the past twenty years, is a history of its president and treasurer; for by his own indefatigable energy and exercise of talent coupled with an exhibition of rare executive ability has the success of the new large factory been attained.

Mr. Monroe is a native of Providence, R.I., where he obtained his early education. When the old Flint Glass Company was started in Meriden by the late Horace C. Wilcox, Mr. Monroe was engaged as a designer by that company. After giving the glass company the benefit of his much appreciated services for some years, he went to Europe. Upon his return from abroad Mr. Monroe opened an art store, the location of which was in the Guy building. In addition to conducting that commendable business he was called upon to do designing by outside parties. The demands made upon him finally became so great that at the end of three or four years that he opened a factory of his own and began the manufacture of decorated glass ware, his first location being on the second floor of the Carter building which adjoined the works of the Meridan Brittania Company on State Street, and where he soon made his name famous in the manufacturing world by putting upon the market a line of decorated goods, most original and attractive, known as "Wave Crest" ware. These goods have ever since been eagerly sought for by buyers in all parts of the United States.

Upon the advice of H.C. Wilcox, in whom he had a most valued friend, Mr. Monroe erected a building on the present site which comprised a two and a half story wooden structure 30 by 62 feet in dimensions.

In 1891 a building three stories in height, 62 by 32 feet, was added by the factory; and the same year the roof of the original building was raised another story, making more than double the original capacity for the busy industry.

In 1900 Mr. Monroe purchased the land next to the factory, extending as far as Main Street, which he caused to be filled in by his concern at a great expense. Again the factory was still further and more noticeably enlarged. The old buildings were separated and moved to a position nearer Main Street, making a building 125 feet long, the whole of which was raised to five stories in height on the old foundations. At this time another, but entirely new building 125 by 30 feet, of three stories, was erected on an angle with the main building. The factory has recently become possessed of an entirely new power plant, with its imposing and stately chimney, which was completed in July, 1905. After the old power house was torn out, the plant was equipped with a large enough engine and boiler and also a generator of sufficient voltage capacity to supply the entire factory not only with electric lights but with motor power for all the different departments.

It was but a few years after Mr. Monroe removed to the present location that glass cutting was added to his output of decorated goods.

A short time after the addition of the cut glass department came that of metal goods. The latest departure of the Monroe Company is the sterling silver deparment which turns out ware unsurpassed either in design or make in this country or Europe.

The factory of the C.F. Monroe Company gives employment to 200 hands, many of whom are accomplished artists, engravers, and designers - necessarily a class of workmen who call for a large weekly payroll on the part of the company. The factory adds more than a little to the prosperity of Meriden and is not only healthfully located, but has been improved to such an extent, both in its artistic interior and attractive grounds, that it is known to the trade as one of the best and neatest kept manufacturing plants in all New England. Its office and show rooms are fitted up artistically and the goods displayed are of such excellence of mechanism and beauty of pattern that the place furnishes a most interesting sight for visitors to frequent. In fact, even the people of Meriden and vicinity are attracted there frequently and seem to take a pardonable pride in showing their friends the dainty articles made there which are so suitable for wedding gifts.

Both the show rooms and offices are more than ordinarily attractive and they have been fitted up and arranged by Mr. Monroe's artistic eye.

Mr. Monroe conducted the business alone until 1892 when, on account of the large increase of business, he found it necessary to form a corporation retaining a large portion of the stock himself and continuing as the active head and holding the offices of both president and treasurer to the present writing. The company is capitalized at $40,000 and the value of the plant represents today an investment of over $200,000.

Mr. Monroe is a member of the Board of Trade and of the general committee of the Meriden Centennial celebration. He is silently interested in several other enterprises besides the concern which bears his name. His efforts in the formation of the Home Club resulted in securing the present club house, and in raising the funds for which he assumed the burden of a great responsibility. Mr. Monroe has been president of the Home Club, of which he is a most valued member, and he is prominent in both social and yachting circles.

He is a member of the Sons of the American Revolution and was one of the founders of the New Bedford Yacht Club, of which he now holds the distinction of being one of the three honorary members. He is also a member of the New York Yacht Club and an ex-commodore of the Pequot Yacht Club of New Haven. Until recently Mr. Monroe owned and sailed the "Sylph", one of the finest schooner yachts on the Atlantic coast.

In 1916 the C.F. Monroe Co. went out of business. Mr. Monroe then became foreman of E. Miller & Co. (in his old factory). They were manufacturers of gas and electric fixtures.

In 1920, Monroe moved to New Hampshire. No other information has been uncovered about his life.

C. F. MONROE CO. FACTORY AND WATERBURY DEPOT, MERIDEN, CONN.

August Schmelzer, Meriden, Conn.

C.F. Monroe Company & His Glass, 1892-1916

My own personal interest in Wave Crest began around 1971 or 1972. On a whim, I visited an antique shop where a beautiful cookie jar caught my eye. It was love at first sight and I bought the lovely jar on the spot. It remains a star in my C.F. Monroe collection today. As time went by and I found myself buying various items of Wave Crest with ever greater interest, I became acquainted with R. Shawn Bradway, a young and serious collector from Connecticut. It soon became apparent that Shawn was tremendously knowledgeable and was probably the earliest and finest dealer in C.F. Monroe glass and other opal ware of quality. I am indebted to him for allowing me to use a pamphlet which he wrote in the mid 1970s, entitled "The C.F. Monroe Story." Shawn has been out of business for almost ten years now, much to the loss of all of us. I have deleted, added, and updated the story as new material has become known. The following then, is the C.F. Monroe Story as we know it today.

Throughout the country, collectors remain keen for the decorated Opal Ware elegancies which were produced at the C.F. Monroe Company in Meriden, Connecticut. Interest in this ware has been building over the past few years, and has now reached fever proportions. Antique dealers are vying for even the simplest pieces, and the rare pieces are practically all now located in the several outstanding collections across the country. With the increasing interest and decreasing supply, prices are soaring.

The C.F. Monroe story is one of the many Cinderella stories of modern day collecting. Until recently, this fine glass was amazingly neglected; amazingly, since it easily rivals similar articles produced by the Smith Brothers and Mt. Washington-Pairpoint Glass Companies in nearby New Bedford, Massachusetts. However, while the demand and the prices began to rise for the various decorated Opal Ware articles produced by Mt. Washington and the Smith Brothers, comparable C.F. Monroe pieces often sat unnoticed on the shelves of many antique shops. All this irrevocably changed when Albert Christian Revi, author of *Ninteenth Century Glass*, and other authors began to call collectors' attention to the fine qualities of this lovely glassware. The fire of collector enthusiasm was ignited, and prices began a dramatic rise.

Decorated Opal Ware was at the height of its popularity from 1890 to 1910, and the C.F. Monroe Company was one of the largest producers of this type glass. Charles F. Monroe opened his first shop in 1880; it was located at 36 West Main Street in Meriden, Connecticut, and he dealt primarily in imported glassware. By 1882, Monroe was operating his own glass decorating studio, and was soon employing highly talented local artists as decorators. When the 1890s arrived and the demand for finely decorated glass was its height, the Monroe company was located in several large buildings on the corner of West Main Street and Capitol Avenue, and employed such fine artists as Carl V. Helmschmied, Walter Nilson, J.J. Knoblauch, Joseph Hickish, Carl Puffee, Flora Feist, Gustave Reinman, Florence Knoblauch, Emil Melchior, and Alma Wenk, Blanche Duval, Gussie Stremlan, Elizabeth Zeibart and Elizabeth Casey. The decorators often went back and forth between the companies, and this sometimes poses a problem of attribution - please see page 173. As is always the case, public tastes changed, and the demand for decorated Opal Ware began to decline after 1910. The C.F. Monroe Company went out of business in 1916.

The Monroe Co. did not manufacture its own glass; rather, it bought its blanks, i.e. undecorated glass, from France, Mt. Washington-Pairpoint and possibly other American glass houses. (One, I was told in personal communication, was Roedifer Glass Co., Bel Air, Ohio. Ray Menendian of Columbus, Ohio, now deceased, knew the son personally. The son had some pieces decorated by C.F. Monroe on glass made by Roedefer.) These glass blanks were of an opaque, creamy white glass called, by the trade, Opal Ware. While the majority of these blanks was made in a mold and the mold lines may be detected on the finished product, pieces have been discovered without any mold marks. I don't think it was ever blown. It is interesting to note that some of the glass, such as the Helmschmied swirl was designed and patented by C.F. Monroe Co. What we now refer to as the egg crate or puffy piece, actually called Billow Ware in the catalogue, as well as the blown out flowers, are unique to C.F. Monroe, as is much of the other glass blanks they used. One can infer that they must have designed the glass, and had it made for them and did not just decorate what was made at the time. It is unusual to see other companies use the same blanks and decorate them.

Before the blanks were decorated, a large number of them were treated to an acid bath of some type; this gave the blanks a soft, lusterless finish. Many of the blanks that were not acidized had a matte surface painted on with the background color. Several acidized pieces have been found with a glossy background color painted on all or part of their surface; these are scarce. Very few pieces were left in their original glossy state.

In C.F. Monroe, the decoration is EVERYTHING. As noted above, there is little art in the glass itself although many of the pieces have interesting and varied shapes. The decoration is mostly very characteristic, as you will see in the pictorial part of the book. Once in a while, a complete surprise comes up (see page 34). The decoration came in at least seven categories or "assortments", as the company called it. (See first page of 1900-1901 catalog). The more intricate the design, the more costly the charge from the factory, and indeed, the more they are worth today. Some of the finest pieces are possibly done in limited numbers and there may have been special orders. The 1900-01 catalog states, "any change from our regular line of stock goods will have to be submitted to the factory, and special prices quoted."

In the decorating process, the majority of the blanks was first entirely or partly painted with one or more background colors in pastel pinks, blues, yellow, and ivory, in rich tones of sage green, apricot, royal blue, and rose, and even in such rarely used colors as purple and black. Some of the skillfully blended colors resemble the earlier Peachblow, Burmese, and other shaded wares; in fact, one combination of pink and yellow so resembles Burmese that it is called "Painted Burmese", and is eagerly sought by collectors. While the background color was being applied, the area which was to be additionally decorated with floral and other motifs had to be kept free from color. This was probably accomplished by applying some type of wax to the design area before the background color was applied. When the background color was fired in the kiln, the wax was burned off, and the area was ready to be decorated.

After the background color was fired, the various motifs were painted on with acid-reduced enamels, usually in delicate colors, and again fired in the kiln. Finally, raised enamel (frequently white), coin gold, enamel and gilt, and raised gold accents were added; this required yet another firing. Those several firings combined with the right artistry, the elaborate decorating techniques, and the fragility of the glass (many pieces were undoubtedly destroyed in the firing process) served to make much of this ware comparatively costly when it was sold.

Floral decor is that which is most frequently encountered on Monroe pieces. Also found are pieces with portraits (especially of Queen Louise), cherubs, and leaf designs. Relatively scarce and in great demand are pieces with seascapes, landscapes, animals, birds, courting couples and geometric, Persian-like, beaded designs. As mentioned previously, all the various motifs were further embellished with white beading, raised gold, lavender scrolls, etc. The total effect was exceedingly rich, bringing to mind the rococo and baroque eras in art.

The C.F. Monroe Company turned out its decorated Opal Ware in a variety of forms. Undoubtedly the most popular was that of a covered, hinged box, and these boxes are found today in an infinite variety of shapes and sizes which include jewelry boxes, oblong glove boxes, etc. Some of these items are in excellent condition and still have the original linings. In addition, today's collector can find Monroe items in such forms as vases, bowls, biscuit jars, pin dishes, card holders, letter holders, etc. Scarce items include sugar sifters, napkin rings, paper weights, whisk broom holders, pin jars, wig holders and blotters, etc. Monroe items, although decorative, were meant to be used. This may be the reason why so few Monroe pieces still exist - they were used, got tarnished, or broken and thrown out.

The majority of Monroe pieces may be divided into three main categories: Wave Crest, Nakara, and Kelva, and pieces may be found with one or the other of these three signatures. Many of the pieces were never signed, especially some of the finest pieces. Monroe frequently stated his belief that the glass "spoke" for itself, and needed no signature. Wave Crest was the first on the market, and enjoyed the largest and longest period of manufacture. Although Wave Crest is generally found with pastel backgrounds and on blanks with elaborate embossing, articles with dark colors and pieces with perfectly plain blanks are occasionally encountered. Wave Crest used a lot of flower transfers, and occasionally scenes and cherubs, etc. They then colored over them, also adding thick enamel touches to make them look hand done. However, it is felt that most of the transfer work came late, when the company tried to save money before it folded. I can only find one transfer piece in the 1900-1901 catalog, page 82, 12-6x. If they made more at that time, they certainly didn't advertise the fact. Wave Crest is found in a much wider variety of shapes and forms than either Nakara or Kelva.

More scarce than Wave Crest, Nakara is frequently found in quite simple shapes with deep, rich background colors accompanied by beaded and raised enamel rococo scrolls. Beading is a characteristic of Nakara, although sometimes a mixture of beading, Nakara pastel backgrounds, and Wave Crest decoration appear on one item. (See B.J. on page 104). Although Nakara is usually found with an acid finish, pieces may be encountered with a glossy surface; these are quite rare. Transfers of portraits, scenes, Gibson Girls, and Kate Greenaway figures are extensively used in Nakara pieces. These are quite beautiful, and command high prices. Occasionally portraits and scenes are fully hand decorated.

Apparently very little Kelva was ever produced, for it is quite infrequently encountered today. Like Nakara, Kelva is generally found in simple shapes; it is always found with its unique, mottled, batik-like background (probably produced by a sponge or crumpled rag dipped in enamel). While Wave Crest and Nakara are found with all types of motifs, Kelva pieces are almost always found with floral decor. Ocassionally, the same blank was used for all three types, and of course there are many exceptions to the above generalizations.

In addition, Monroe produced four other categories of decorated glass. One is a type of decorated crystal glass with enamel stained background quite similar to, and frequently mistaken for Mt. Washington Royal Flemish and Verona in the finest pieces. Monroe's Decorated Crystal Ware may be found in the same shapes and with the same decor as the Opal Ware pieces or may be found in entirely different shapes and entirely different decorations. Quite a few of the Decorated Crystal Ware items have the raised white beading found on so much of the Opal Ware. When signed, these pieces have the Wave Crest black mark signature.

The second type is a decorated Opal Ware quite similar in coloring to Nakara, but with bisque-like china flowers applied to the glass. Very rare pieces with both portraits and applied flowers can occasionally be found; these are generally of exceptional beauty, and are usually signed Nakara.

Like Mt. Washington, Monroe produced some pieces which could be called Blown-out Opal Ware, and this is the third type. Essentially, some part of the blank is so raised as to appear blown-out like the Pairpoint lamps of that name. On some Monroe pieces, the blown-out portions were enameled in such a way as to accent their raised position. The Monroe Company turned out unusual small boxes in which the top was almost entirely covered by an exquisitely tinted, blown-out flower. These blown-out pieces may be found with one of Monroe's identifying signatures in all three lines.

The fourth is Wave Crest Cameo. The opal ware boxes were cut back with a pattern and then painted to outline the design. The bottom half of the box was also cut to finish out the design with the top. These boxes are exceedingly rare. I have tried to show one before it was painted, but it didn't come out, as it was all white (see page 18).

Many Monroe collectors are not aware that the C.F. Monroe Company produced cut glass. Around the turn of the century, they produced some of the finest cut glass in the country; unfortunately, very few pieces were marked. However, Monroe cut glass boxes can be easily recognized because they generally take the same shape and have the same collars and clasps as their Opal Ware counterparts. Even less well known is the fact that this same company manufactured some beautifully embossed sterling silver and brass boxes. Now and then an article of cut glass with a marked "sterling" part and, occasionally, signed with "C.F.M. Co." or a trademark will come to light.

Once in a great while, a piece of finely decorated china will be discovered bearing the signature of some Monroe artist; it is highly doubtful that these pieces were production items. These china pieces frequently have the same type of decoration as found on Wave Crest (see page 71) and include cake plates, dishes, ash trays, etc. Also see 1895 catalog page 175.

The majority of Monroe articles are found with silverplated or ormolu metal parts attached to them. Some pieces have brass parts and these can sometimes be found with "CFM Co." signed on the piece. While ormolu parts are found on a majority of the items, silverplated parts are usually found on table items such as biscuit jars, sugar sifters, salt and peppers, etc. and on quite a few of the Kelva pieces. The metal parts were attached to the glass with plaster of paris. (When making any repairs, do not ever attach them with any form of glue. They will never come off again!)

In conclusion, a few words should be given to the "problem" of signatures. While many of Monroe's most commercial pieces were signed, a large number of the finest pieces, especially in the Wave Crest line, were not signed. (They may have had paper labels). These unsigned beauties have far greater aesthetic worth and eventually will have a far greater value than the simple, signed pieces. I have often seen collectors leave a beautiful piece because it was unsigned. In my own opinion, the signature is totally unnecessary in 99.9% of C.F. Monroe glass, and does not make the piece worth more or less. The glass and decoration are usually so distinctive, to even the early collector, that it can easily be recognized as a piece of C.F. Monroe. For those who are unsure, I can only say, as in all fields of collecting, get to know your subject. I hope this book will help in that regard. Rarely, in my experience, but once in a great while, items with forged signatures appear, usually with the banner mark, and this should serve to further discourage an over-reliance on signatures. The forged mark will usually wash right off. Finally, there is no evidence of one signature being any earlier than the other. As Monroe himself believed, his glass does speak for itself, and no serious student of glass needs a signature, true or otherwise, "early" or "late", in identifying the elegancies produced by this fine company.

A word on identification: Sometimes, I am not sure if a piece is C.F. Monroe (see page 48). If you are not sure, make the seller justify their attribution. It's not enough for them to say "If you've handled as much glass as I have over the years," etc. That doesn't explain anything, and proves nothing except that they really don't know. Most reliable dealers are eager to help by discussing the pros and cons of obscure pieces, and especially will admit if they are in the dark about an item. None of us know it all, and we stand to learn a great deal from each other.

A final note: Not all opal glass, with or without rococo was Monroe. Some of the pieces confusing to novices are other manufacturers' forms of Opal Ware, probably Belle Ware, Handel (page 172) or Keystone Ware (page 173) and not necessarily Monroe.

Signatures

As stated elsewhere, and I feel it is so important, that I feel it is necessary to repeat: the signature is unimportant in making a decision on whether or not to buy a piece of C.F. Monroe. IT DOES NOT ADD TO THE VALUE. The value is based on the quality of decoration, and of course, the rarity. The signatures are placed here for completeness of this book.

TRADE **KELVA.** MARK

TRADE WAVE CREST. MARK

C.F.M.Co.

Rare signature on glass.
Similar signature on metal,
but "o" is of equal size.

C.F.M.CO.
NAKARA

NAKARA
C.F.M.CO.

Wave Crest Cameo and Blown Out

Large footed octagon CAMEO cut box with original Wave Crest paper label. Scene is then painted on raised areas. Top shows clouds and waves, or ripples, which can be seen under gondola. Bottom part of box is cut and painted to show water on front and back, and seaweed on sides. Box on right is fully cut. Base has different cut. I'm sorry it didn't show better. 4½″ x 8½″.

Left: Overall Cameo cut box with winter scene of lamb and a fox. Bottom is also cut. 6″ diameter. Right: Hand-painted Venetian scene on round raised rococo box. 3¾″ diameter.

Three small boxes: Left: Lovely and unusual wheel house scene, hand painted. Middle: Rare aster in blow-out. Right: Rare cameo cut in sailing scene. 3¾″ diameter. Newland collection.

Two Wave Crest cameo boxes with ships and water. Right is artist signed "Kuttonia". Neale-Schlotfeldt collection.

Wave Crest Blow-outs: Left: Rose on lid with hand-painted roses on bottom to match. 4″ diameter. Middle: Pansy on lid in unusual shiny "marbelized" brown color. Right: Unusual maple leaf on lid. 4″ diameter.

Left & Right: Two tobacco humidors. 5¼″ tall. Middle: Blown-out zinnia in cobalt blue. 5″ diameter.

Largest Wave Crest blown-out, in cobalt blue. Rare. This box is also seen in green in the crystal section of this book. I have seen this latter color a few times. Neale-Schlotfeldt collection.

Wave Crest Perfumes, Bon-Bons, Ferners, Jardinieres, and Salt and Pepper Shakers

Left: Large bon-bon. 6¾″ diameter. Right: Medium bon-bon. These are quite hard to find. 1½″ x 5¼″.

Covered bon-bon dish comes in two sizes - rare. Bonnie & Jack Duprey collection.

Two medium bon-bons. Satin and shiny finishes on both. 1½″ x 5¼″.

Covered bon-bons. They don't appear in any catalogs, but I'm sure the lids are original. Probably quite rare.

Bon-bon with unusual brass lid. Brinkman collection.

Two Wave Crest ferners in different blanks.

Two Wave Crest ferners. Right one is unique to me.

Left: Blank is quite rare. Right: Footed. Blank is hard to find. Unusual floral panels. 3½″ x 7¾″.

Medium ferneries in two different shapes. Liners are missing. #1. 5″ square; #2. 5½″ diameter.

Ferneries, footed, with liners. 2½″ x 7¼″.

Rare jardinieres, one beaded along rim edge and the other with a line of applied gold trim. 7″ tall.

Planter, transfer. 7½″ tall.

Large planter, hand painted. Most of these blanks are transfers. 7½″ tall.

Very hard to find footed jardiniere with rolled metal rim. They came with different rims and occasionally without feet. 6½″ tall.

Rare footed jardiniere (slightly different blank), 6½″ tall. Newland collection.

Salts: Left pair: Hand-painted "Creased Neck". Right pair: Hard to find without worn decoration.

Salts: from left: #1 & #2 are hand-painted "Tulip" and same as biscuit jar. Most tulips are transfers. #3 & #4 are called "Spear" and have cats on transfer. #5 is a hard to find Wave Crest salt with sterling top which might not be original. #6 & #7 are "woven" in neck. Also hard to find. Left one has a cat on transfer.

Salts: Left two are Mt. Washington blanks, but the decoration is 100% Wave Crest. The next four are called "Wave Crest Salts" in the catalog - Erie Twist commonly now. #3 has a fish front and back. #5 & #6 are in the rare russet color.

Hand-decorated Wave Crest salts: Left: #1, #2 & #3 are now named "Scroll". #3 is beautiful with roses and gold trim. #4 & #5 are the same blank (#5 lacks a top - but is easily the finest Wave Crest salt I've seen). #6 is a slightly different blank.

Wave Crest salts: #2, #3 & #4 are transfers, and #2 & #4 have a bird on a branch.

Wave Crest salts: Outside pairs are identical and called "Billow" by the company. Middle two are unusual and square, and look much like the biscuit jars of the same shape; top on left one is probably original.

Salts: Left: Believe it or not, these are signed with the Wave Crest black mark. If it wasn't for my wife's intuition, I would never have picked them up. Nothing looks less like Wave Crest than these to me. Middle two: Daisy salts, named by the company - 1895-96 catalog. #5 probably made by Wave Crest. Worn transfer top says "Meriden Centennial 1906." Bottom: "Merry - Den Tavern", with a picture of two buildings between. #6 is rare with shells on both sides.

Two pair of salts: Exceptional decoration on both. The pair on the left is extremely rare, and appears to be similar to the "parker salt" on page 86 of 1900-01 catalog. This pair, however, has a standard top. Newland collection.

Left: Sugar shaker, with alternating yellow and pink panels. Right: Pair of scroll salts with rare cobalt blue. Andes collection.

Left & Right: Stoppered colognes. Middle: Atomizer. Neale-Schlotfeldt collection.

Left: Cigarette humidor in cobalt blue. Middle: Lovely hair receiver in cobalt. Right: Unusual cologne dug up in Meriden, Connecticut. Coutermash collection.

Left: Atomizer. Right: Covered piece in frame. Might be either a candy dish or pickle castor. Lyle collection.

Four outstanding atomizers with exceptional decoration. Any one would be a prize to own. Note unusual gold beading on right. Newland collection. #1. 4¼″ x 3¾″; #2. 3¾″ x 2½″.

From left: #1 & #4 are *bud* vases. They never had stoppers. #2 & #3 are atomizer perfumes. #1. & #2. 4½″ x 4″; #3. 2½″ x 3½″; #4. 3¾″ x 2½″.

Back row: left: Rare cologne with opal stopper, 5¼″ x 4¼″. Right: Rare cologne with clear glass stopper under silver cap, 4¼″ x 3¾″. Front row: left: Hand-painted atomizer. Center: Transfer atomizer. Right: Helmschmied Swirl (hardware missing), 4¼″ tall.

Wave Crest Vases

Five bud vases: Left: Shell motif. Right two: Most unusual decoration, lack rims. They are identical, with one turned 90°. Many people have thought these were colognes with lost stoppers - they never had them. See reprint of 1900-01 supplement. #1. 2¼″ x 3¼″; #2. 1¾″ x 3¼″; #3. 2½″ x 3¼″.

Outside pair: Squatty vases with feet. Unusual lines of color. Beaded rims. 3¾″ x 4¼″. Inside pair: Footed vases, 6¼″ x 3½″.

Five small Wave Crest vases. From left: #2 & #4 are the same blanks, fine decoration on #4. #3 is different blank. #3. 5¼″ x 2¼″; #5. 3″ x 2″.

From left: #1. Unusual bud vase, 3″ x 2″; #2. Double shell bud vase, 2¼″ x 3¼″; #3. Rare match holder; #4. Unusual vase, note the decoration at base. Newland collection.

From left: #1, #3, #4 & #6 are "vase ornaments". #4 has its handles "twisted", and #6 has its bottom glass upside down. #2 & #5 are small vases with the latter finished in beads (without metal rim). #1. 5¾" tall; #2. 3¼" x 1¾".

Four medium vases: two are finished in beads on rim. The first time I saw the "lines" of paint, (that three of these have), I thought someone had experimented post factory! #1. 5½" x 2¼"; #2. 6" x 3"; #3. 8" x 3¾"; #4. 5¾" x 3¼".

Outside pair: Wave Crest vases in unusual blank (see Kelva section), 7½″ x 3″. Inside pair: Footed Vases with beaded rims, (these also came without feet), 9″ x 3″.

Exceptional vase in unusual blue background. Quite rare. Approx. 15″ tall. Newland collection.

Intricately decorated pair of vases with bottoms shown in next photo. Signed by artist J.J. Knoblauck, June, 1894. I have never seen other Wave Crest artist signed. Dee's Antiques collection.

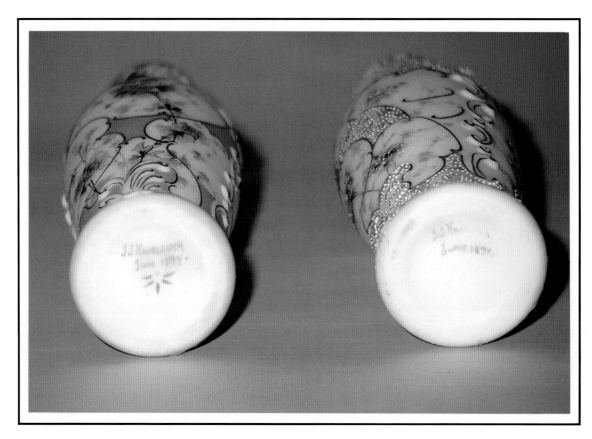

Top Left: Unusual large vase with birds in flight. Approx. 15″ tall. Brinkman collection.

Top right: A spectacular hand-painted vase in cobalt blue with unusual handles. Very rare. Flowers (mums) on back. 11¼″ x 4″.

Bottom right: Two Wave Crest vases in different colors and flowers, done in cameo effect. Note missing foot on left vase. These vases originally had long handles attached to metal rim. 13½″ x 5″.

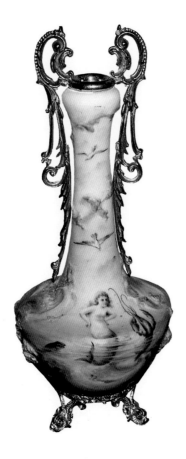

Top left: Vase with mermaid in sea. Note unusual handles. Grimmer collection.

Top right: Same as vases below but with unusual decoration of ribbons. Andes collection.

Bottom left: A pair of vases: One on left has had part of handles broken off. Also made in crystal. 10½″ x 3¾″.

Left: Absolutely wonderful hand-painted vase with dark glossy green finish. Scene is "Mary had a little lamb". 10¾″ x 4¾″. Newland collection. Note: Both vases are missing their rim hardware.

A pair of Wave Crest vases with different backgrounds. Note finished beaded top on left vase. Right vase has had its rim painted, and probably had a metal fitting at one time. 10¾″ x 4¾″.

Vase with hand-painted ships in panel. Note missing metal foot. This is so unusual it is worth having without the foot. 10¾″ x 4¾″.

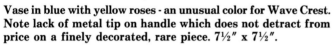

Vase in blue with yellow roses - an unusual color for Wave Crest. Note lack of metal tip on handle which does not detract from price on a finely decorated, rare piece. 7½″ x 7½″.

Wave Crest vase in unusual hand-painted design with rare deep rust color. 9″ x 6½″.

Wave Crest vase in panels of flowers. 9″ x 6½″.

Wave Crest with flower design. All six of these have exceptional hand-painted decor. Lyle collection.

Wave Crest vase in an almost cameo simulated effect. 9″ x 6½″.

Hand-painted Wave Crest vase. Andes collection.

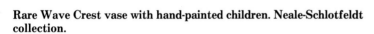

Rare Wave Crest vase with hand-painted children. Neale-Schlotfeldt collection.

Hand-painted Wave Crest vase. Rare rust color.

Rare hand-painted Wave Crest vase with lovely lady and cherubs. The painting is as fine as any oil on canvas. Rear panel has pastoral scene. 12″ x 8½″.

Large vase - back panel of vase with lady and cherubs.

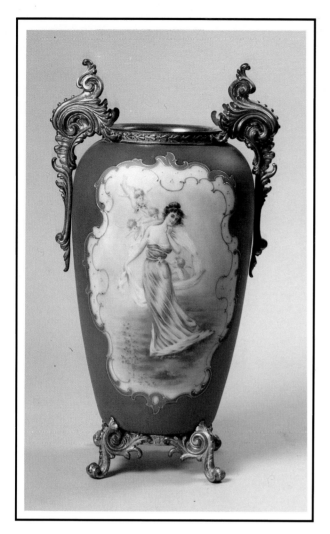

Large vase in blue, 12″ x 8½″. Newland collection.

Large vase - back panel is almost the same as front. Jet black in shiny finish. 12″ x 8½″.

Large vase - back panel is similar to front. Very dark green in shiny finish. 12″ x 8½″.

Large vase with unusually fine hand-painted scene. Dark green glossy finish. 12″ x 8½″. Newland collection.

Absolutely gorgeous vase with hand-painted orchids. As fine as any painting on canvas. 12″ x 8½″.

Large vase in pastel blue. Lyle collection.

Two large vases: Ladies are transfers, and the rest is hand painted. Unsigned. These were sold to me as Wave Crest and Shawn Bradway had a pamphlet with one pictured and stated it was Wave Crest. I've looked at them for a great deal of time, many times. I can't convince myself 100% that they are Wave Crest and yet I don't know what else to call them. I hope someone can put me out of my misery. 14¼″ tall.

Wave Crest Crystal

Left: Large opal box. Right: Identical large box, but in crystal. Nine storks and setting sun on lid. Gold and panelled colors are quite similar to Royal Flemish. Extremely rare. 7″ diameter.

Left: Medium box in crystal. Extremely rare. Right: Medium box in Opal Ware. Seven storks on lid. 5½″ diameter.

Left: Large opal box with rare violet color. Right: Large crystal box. 7″ diameter.

Three crystal boxes: These are all identical to opal boxes. Left: Mostly satinized with one clear panel with florals. 3¼″ x 4¼″. Middle: Lovely satin blue box with florals. 8″ diameter. Right: Unusual pink color. All crystal boxes were lined originally. 5½″ diameter.

Left: Rare large, shiny crystal box in classical Helmschmied Swirl. The design is very intricate and unusual. I have not seen another box in this color. Right: Same box in satin crystal with holly. It is said that these were made for Christmas. 7″ diameter.

Wave Crest box in crystal. Note tiny beading on top. 3½″ tall x 7″ deep. Black mark signature. Brinkman collection.

Two medium crystal boxes in yellow and blue (see pink, this section). Neale-Schlotfeldt collection.

Left: Similar to crystal box with beading. Signed. Right: Lavender crystal watch box, signed. Lyle collection.

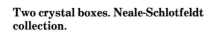

Two crystal boxes. Neale-Schlotfeldt collection.

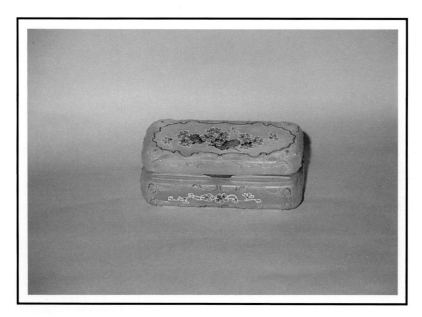

Lovely crystal glove box with exceptional decoration. 10″ x 4¼″. Unfortunately, hardware is missing. Lyle collection.

Left: Crystal vase. Right: Extremely rare crystal water carafe. Neale-Schlotfeldt collection.

Another cigar band crystal box. Only two I've ever seen. Neale-Schlotfeldt collection.

Left: Extremely rare, non-satin crystal box, lined with cigar bands in lid and on sides. Original satin lining in lid and bottom like other Wave Crest boxes. 5¾″ diameter. Right: The largest blown-out Wave Crest box made. Hand-painted flowers on side to match the top. It is a beauty and a favorite of mine. A friend saw it and thought it was a decorated cake. 7¾″ diameter.

Wave Crest Mirror Trays, Clocks, Plates and Candlesticks

Largest mirror tray made. Relined by my wife. She has figured out the mathematical formula needed to reline them (and the boxes) in the original way. 9¾″ x 7½″.

Medium mirror tray. This is the only one I have ever seen with an oval mirror. 9½″ x 4½″. Newland collection.

Three different mirror trays. Only the center one has the original lining. When the linings left the factories, they were scented, according to the catalogs, but they never said what scent! #1. 6″ diameter; #2. 4″ diameter; #3. 5¼″ diameter.

Left: Clock box, 3″ x 5″. Right: Easel clock. Easel is gone, so it makes an excellent wall clock 8¾″ overall. All clocks for Wave Crest were made by Waterbury Clock Co.

Easel clock in cobalt blue color. This is the nicest one I've seen. 8¾″ overall. Newland collection.

Easel clock with rare triangular Ormalu fitting. Newland collection.

Left: Clock box in a different blank. Right: Unusual-shaped covered box.

Opal plate - unsigned. It said Wave Crest to me instantly. See scene on vase on page 3 of 1895-96 catalog. 11½″ x 8¾″.

Rare rectangular hand-painted plate. 11″ x 7½″. Newland collection.

Wave Crest charger, transfer, unsigned, shiny, probably done late in company's lifetime. 11″ diameter.

Lovely hand-painted plate, rare. 11″ diameter. Newland collection.

Wave Crest candlesticks. Left: One of two blanks made. Right: A "pair", even though of different colors. They were sold singly, and this may be the reason for pairs existing in unmatched colors. I'd love to know why they are so rare. 7″ overall.

A pair of candlesticks in blue and pink. 7″ overall. Newland collection.

Left: Bottom half of match box holder. Right: Candlestick holder, very rare. Only one I've seen. Neale-Schlotfeldt collection.

Three decorated trays. Quite worn decorations. Probably Wave Crest. Lyle collection.

Wave Crest Table Items

Unusual set in transfer with hand-painted colors. Biscuit jar, spooner, syrup and creamer. Purchased separately.

Left three: Matching creamer, sugar and spooner. Difficult to find all three. Right: Creamer and sugar.

Wave Crest: Creamer and sugar. Left: This has been called Crown Milano and Belle Ware. I was sure it was Wave Crest, but couldn't prove it until I saw page 22 of the 1895-96 catalog. Right: Early decoration.

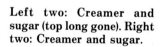

Left two: Creamer and sugar (top long gone). Right two: Creamer and sugar.

Table set in transfer pattern of toadstools. Lyle collection.

From left: #1. Unusual and rare pickle castor. Different hardware for Wave Crest; #2. Early sugar shaker; #3. Covered sugar; #4. Rare (transfer) syrup, signed. Only one I've seen. Glass handle. Newland collection.

From left: #1. and #4. are extremely rare pickle jars. See page 31 of 1895-96 catalog. I bought these in a frame, but as you can see they never came that way. 4½″ x 3″. #2. Sugar sifter; #3. Syrup (hard to find), 4¼″ x 2¾″.

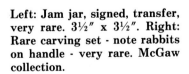

Left: Jam jar, signed, transfer, very rare. 3½″ x 3½″. Right: Rare carving set - note rabbits on handle - very rare. McGaw collection.

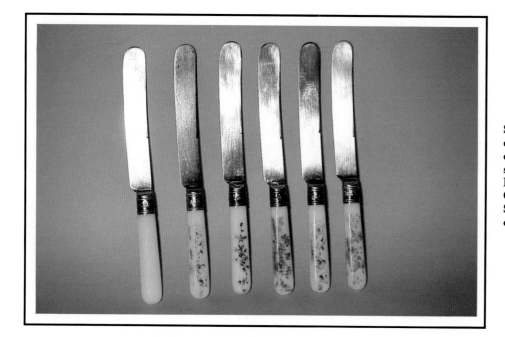

Set of six knives: One is plain, one is hand painted, and the others have transfers of chicks, sunbonnet babies and a house. Blades are engraved "Goodell Company, Antrim, N.H. Pat. Sept. 8, 1904." Neale-Schlotfeldt collection.

From left: Back: #1. Mustard; #2. Sugar shaker (early decoration); #3. Mustard - both are quite rare. The catalog shows only two mustards; #4. Finger bowl with matching plate (extremely rare). Transfer. See page 34 of 1895-96 catalog. Front: #1. Rare butter pat, transfer; #2. Pin receiver, very rare. See page 14 of 1895-96 catalog; #3. Open salt; #4. Toothpick; #5. Rare Wave Crest napkin ring; #6. Sugar shaker.

Left three: Matched hand-painted salt and pepper and mustard. Although the salt and pepper are shown in the catalog, they are the only ones I have seen in this blank. The mustards alone are extremely difficult to find in my experience. Right two: Salt and pepper decoration is certainly Wave Crest. The only ones I have seen in this blank. Lyle collection.

Left: Syrup. Right: Rare shiny condiment set in (probably) original holder. Neale-Schlotfeldt collection.

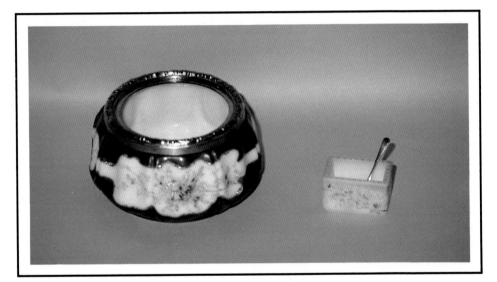

Left: Medium cobalt ferner. Right: Extremely rare rectangular open salt. I knew about it, only from the 1895-96 catalog, and a long story goes with its acquisition. Suffice it to say that I know of no others even though they were sold by the dozen. I have talked to two dealers on the east coast who only deal in open salts and they have never seen or heard of one.

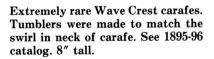

Extremely rare Wave Crest carafes. Tumblers were made to match the swirl in neck of carafe. See 1895-96 catalog. 8″ tall.

Carafe and six tumblers. All extremely rare in my experience. Two different tumblers are shown in 1895-96 catalog, but I have never been able to find one for sale. Neale-Schlotfeldt collection.

Pitcher and two tumblers. These are outstanding pieces with intricate decoration, and no photo can do them justice. Decoration is very similar to signed vase by J.J. Knoblauck seen elsewhere in book. Lyle collection.

Rare pitcher with classic Wave Crest decoration. Neale-Schlotfeldt collection.

Whisk broom holder.

Broom holder.

From left: Spittoon, toothpick and syrup. All have identical decoration to confirm attribution. McGaw collection.

Left: Wave Crest spittoon, unsigned. Right: Wave Crest celery (?) vase, unsigned. I bought the vase first. I have looked and looked at it, trying to convince myself it was Wave Crest and not Mt. Washington. Then I bought the spittoon and went through the same thing all over again. Finally I saw the McGaw's collection, and I was sure it was Wave Crest.

This rare piece is shown two ways: Left: With stopper, and said to be a cruet. Right: Without stopper as a bud vase. 6″ tall. It appears in 1900-01 supplememt on page 8 as a bud vase. It doesn't appear in any extant literature with a stopper and this may have been added later. Help!!! Newland collection.

Wave Crest Umbrella Stands, Urns, Brass Boxes, French Clocks and Candlesticks, China, and Lamps

Umbrella stand. Note different hardware top and bottom. These are panels of pastel colors. Very rare. Approx. 22″ tall overall. Newland collection.

Matching pair of hand-painted urns.

Two exceptionally rare brass boxes - small and medium in size. Both signed: "C.F.M. Co." Newland collection.

I looked at this for ½ to ¾ of an hour before deciding to buy it. The glass at the top is definitely Wave Crest. The glass panel near the bottom is cherubs in a transfer. But it was the clock itself which sold me. Made by Waterbury Clock Co. U.S.A. This is the company that made all Wave Crest clock boxes and easels. I have since seen a clock almost identical, except it did not have the glass piece on top. Then when I saw the Newlands' candlesticks I was positive it was Wave Crest. 14″ tall to top of finial.

Exceptionally rare candlesticks. Note glass panels in base with pastoral scenes. A match for the clock. These and the clock were bought years apart. I have also seen these in a "branched" candelabra. Newland collection.

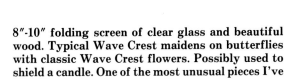

China tray with C.F.M. flowers signed in left corner "F.K." for Flora Knoblauck, wife of J. Knoblauck. 5¼" square.

8"-10" folding screen of clear glass and beautiful wood. Typical Wave Crest maidens on butterflies with classic Wave Crest flowers. Possibly used to shield a candle. One of the most unusual pieces I've seen. Dee's Antiques collection.

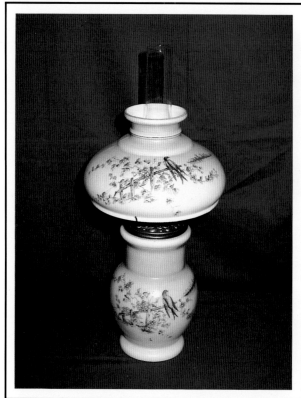

Lamp with "Bird on a Fence" transfer. McGaw collection.

Lamp appears to be Wave Crest decoration. 12″ Andes collection.

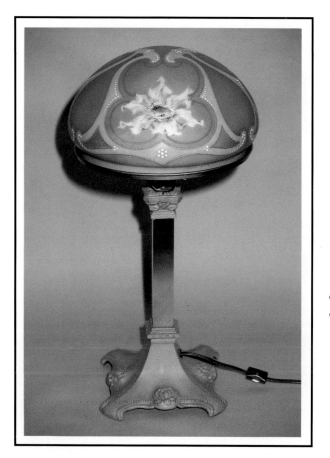

This lamp has been traced positively to the factory. Nakara decoration. Andes collection.

Wave Crest Clerical Items

From left: #1. Extremely rare ink stand, in lime green. An opalescent, milk glass ink holder inside. 4½″ tall overall; #2. Footed spindle, or "memo-file" as the company called them. 7½″ tall overall; #3. Spindle; #4. Ink well, rare, different shape than in the 1900-01 catalog. I have never seen the latter. See 1900-01 catalog supplement. 3¾″ tall x 4″; #5. Blotter, rare, comes in three different blanks. 2¾″ tall overall x 5¼″ long.

Left: Rare, footed paperweight with cherub. Middle: Card holder in unusual blank. Note intact lining. Right: Paperweight. Newland collection.

Left: Footed photo receiver. Middle: Photo receiver. Right: Card holder with transfer of Niagra Falls. (I once saw one of these with the original deck of cards with scenes of the Falls on the cards.)

Left: Early photo receiver, footed. Middle: Photo receiver. Right: Playing card holder.

Left: Footed photo receiver elaborately decorated. Right: Rare match box holder. McGaw collection.

Blotters in pastel yellow and blue, very rare. Newland collection.

Left: Extremely rare whist bonbon bell. Note bell thumb activator to right of left hand; domed glass to accept the mechanism for the bell. I have also seen this tray (domed) without the mechanism (rusted and thrown out?). 8″ diameter. Right: Hard to find call bell. 3½″ overall x 4¾″.

Left three: Originally, I was told that these were a napkin ring set. However, I am sure that they are part of a smoke set, and were attached to a metal (or wood) base. Right: Paperweight with cherub and cymbals. 3″ tall. McGaw collection.

Left: Footed tray - new lining. Right: Footed photo receiver with unusual green background.

Very rare footed ink well with glass insert. Grimmer collection.

Exceedingly rare fan-shaped photo receiver. Metal base is probably not original. Only one I've ever seen. Pictured in back of C.F. Monroe cut glass catalog. Dee's Antiques collection.

Wave Crest Tobacco and Smoking Accessories

Left: Humidor with Indian on horseback with bow drawn. 6½″ x 5″. Right: Biscuit jar, unusual form without bail. McGaw collection.

Left: Cigar humidor with lock. This base is also made in rarely found biscuit jar. 6½″ x 5″. Right: Cigar humidor with blown-out shell on lid. 5¾″ x 4″.

Two humidors: Left: Small size for cigarettes in unusual green. Right: Large with key lock in rare lime green color. 6″ x 5″. Newland collection.

Left: Cigar set, side holders for matches. Middle: Match box, extremely rare. Right: Match safe, exceptionally rare. See 1895-96 catalog for authentication. This is not a toothpick holder, unfortunately for toothpick fans. The signature on the bottom of each of the glass pieces are signed differently than any other glass piece I've ever seen. "C.F.M. Co.". The metal pieces are sometimes signed similarly, but the letters are smaller and the "o" is equal in size, as it is in the Nakara signature. 4¼″ x 1¼″.

Left: Wall mounted match box holder (being held by plate holder). 1½″ x 4″ x 2½″. Right: Paperweight. These are extremely hard to find. 1″ x 3″.

Three different ash receivers or jewel trays. 1¼″ x 3″.

Back left: #1."Combination ash tray and match holder". See 1900-01 supplement, page 20 (page 231); Back #2. & #3. Cigar holders; Front left: This little fellow is very rare and has caused much controversy and discussion. As you see on page 19 of 1900-01 supplement (page 230), it is a match holder, and not a toothpick holder. An original catalog is wonderful to settle issues. Front right: Match holder. #1. 1½" x 5½"; #2. 1¾" x 2¼"; #3. 2¼" x 2¾"; #4. 1¼" x 1¾".

Three humidors: Left and right for cigars. "Cigars" appears on *back* of one on left. #1. 4¾" x 3½"; #2. 3¾" tall; #3. 5¾" x 4". Newland collection.

Left: Smoke set consisting of match holder and ash receiver. These combinations are quite rare. Right: Tobacco humidor. Lyle collection.

Left: Smoke set on metal base. Right: Tobacco humidor with owl. Neale-Schlotfeldt collection.

Smoke set with ornate metal base. I have seen these sets ocassionally on original wood bases.

Wave Crest Boudoir Items

Very rare "Whisk broom or comb and brush case". This was hung on the wall and had small curtains from rails on sides to cover opening of Opal Ware glass cylinder. 6″ x 4¼″, glass, only.

Comb and brush case wall hanging. Light blue shading. Opal cylinder was originally lined with satin. Note original curtain rings on brass rail above the opening that held a tie-back curtain. See 1895-96 catalog, page 19. Newland collection.

Dresser box with tray. Boxes are part of tray. One box is fully lined. The other has metal bottom lining it. 10″ x 8″.

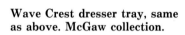 Wave Crest dresser tray, same as above. McGaw collection.

Left: Hair receiver. Right: Medium bishop hat is made into biscuit jar. This mold virtually always appears in Nakara. 6¾″ diameter. Newland collection.

Left: Extremely rare pin cushion and tray. Probably all original. Right: Extremely rare and gorgeous whiskey flask. This was also made in cut glass. See 1900-01 supplement, page 18. Newland collection.

From top left: #1. Trinket, comb and brush holder. Relatively hard to find. This is a very decorative piece. #2. Lady's flask, unsigned. A prominent dealer also feels this is Wave Crest, but I give no 100% guarantee. Bottom: #1. Footed pin tray, rare. #2. Pin tray. Note holes in ends. This may have been a candlestick holder. See page 11 of 1895-96 catalog. #3. Extremely rare hair receiver, signed. Metal piece just lays on top and does not fit in the bottom. I almost walked by this, but it spoke to me, and I almost fell over when I turned it upside down.

From left: #1. & #2. Very hard to find toothbrush holders. Any top will do as original ones are mostly gone. I believe original top is the same as on bottom row, #3 below. #3. Ring box, signed, extremely rare in Wave Crest I believe it to be original. Unique to me. #1. & #2. 6¾″ tall. Bottom: #1. Open pomade with ring handles I believe to be original. Unique to me. #2. Hair receiver. Getting hard to find. #3. Very rare small pomade box. #4. Hard to find pomade box. #5. Tooth powder box. Note insert that fits in top to limit tooth powder. The insert is very rare, as most have been lost. Worth having anyway, without insert. #1. 1¾″ tall; #3. 1¼″ tall; #4. 1¾″ tall; #5. 3″ tall.

Wave Crest Boxes

Four small boxes: Different combinations of lids and bottoms were used to give an infinite variety to the boxes. #1. 3½″ square; #2. 3″ square.

Four different small boxes. Second from left is a transfer, and probably from the later period. 3″ to 4″.

Three boxes: Left and far right are cherub transfers with hand-painted colors and florals. Middle is a transfer of a bridge scene. #1. & #3.: 4″ diameter; #2. 3½″ diameter.

Three boxes: Left: Blown-out shell, 4″ diameter. Middle: Rectangular egg crate, 5¾″ x 3¼″. Right: Double shell, 3″ diameter.

Three boxes: Far right is footed with blown-out shell on lid. Bottom is different than the other shell box pictured. #1. 5″ diameter; #2. 5″ square; #3. 4″ diameter.

Left: Oval box with transfer of cherubs and mountain scene, 5″L. Middle: Medium box with transfer of couple (man on bended knee - must be from a long time past). 5½″ diameter. Right: Small box with child in sun bonnet. Transfer, 3″ diameter. Newland collection.

Three boxes of various shapes and colors. I call the middle one "Limoges" because the painting gives the look of china on first glance. I have not seen another like it. #1. 5½″; #2. 4¾″ diameter; #3. 4″ tall x 5″ square.

Three boxes of various shapes. #1. & #3. 3½″ diameter; #2. 5″ diameter.

Three boxes: Left and far right use same blank for bottom and lid. Note similarity, except for extra rococo on right hand one. Popular oval box in center. #1. 2½″ tall x 5″ square; #2. 5½″ diameter; #3. 2½″ tall x 5″ square.

Three medium boxes in different colors and hand-painted designs. Note popular Wave Crest fern design on left. 5″ diameter.

Three boxes of varying shapes. Footed pieces of all kinds are harder to find and thus worth more. The metal is very soft and breaks easily. Then it is thrown out and only the box survives. #1. 5″ diameter; #2. 5″ square; #3. 5¾″ tall.

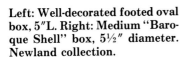

Left: Well-decorated footed oval box, 5″L. Right: Medium "Baroque Shell" box, 5½″ diameter. Newland collection.

Two Wave Crest boxes with cherub transfers on lids. #1. 5″ square; #2. 5¼″ diameter.

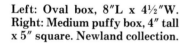

Left: Oval box, 8″L x 4½″W. Right: Medium puffy box, 4″ tall x 5″ square. Newland collection.

Left: Square footed box with roses on lid, 6″L x 5″W. Right: A hard to find oval footed box with an almost blown-out effect on top and sides. This one is a very dark green, but it comes in other colors. One of my favorites. This may be the kind of glass that gave the company its name. It's said that the rococo on the glass looks like waves and hence "Wave Crest". That explanation may be far fetched. 8″L x 4¼″W.

Left: Medium square box with rose on lid, 6″ x 5″. Right: Rare blank, 7½″L. Newland collection.

Two medium boxes: Left: Footed with key lock. Unusual blank. #1. 7″ diameter; #2. 6½″ square. Newland collection.

Two boxes of identical shape and decoration in different sizes. Two maidens walking in woods. Hand painted. #1. 6½″ square; #2. 5″ square. Newland collection.

Two egg crate humidors. These have removable metal plate in top to hold sponge. Left: Medium size tobacco, 4″ tall x 5″ square. Right: Large size cigars, 6½″ square.

Left: Beautiful, footed, locked box with raised unpainted florals on lid, 7″ diameter. Right: A most beautiful cigar humidor with lock and hand-painted maiden on the lid. Rear panel has hand-painted roses, 6″ tall.

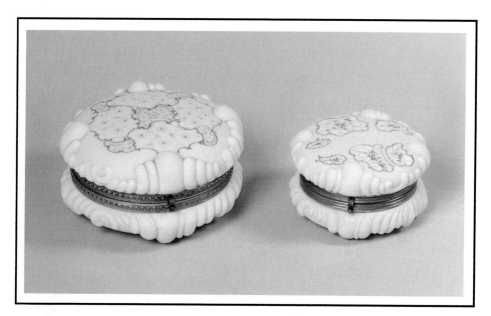

Left: Large Baroque shell box, 7″ diameter. Right: Medium box, 5½″ diameter.

Two large boxes in Helms-chmied Swirl. 7″ diameter.

Wave Crest box with fish. Very unusual. 4½″ tall x 6″ diameter. Brinkman collection.

Very early Wave Crest decoration with unusual overall florals, done by not coloring flowers. Note whimsical barking dogs (in a manner similar to Royal Flemish) in heavy gold. Left: Sugar shaker. Right: Large box, 7″ diameter.

Medium box with fish and shells on lid. Gilliam collection.

Large footed box with metal bottom instead of glass. The first time I saw this I thought it was a repair, but it is correct, and from the factory. 7″ diameter. Newland collection.

Unusual footed collars and cuffs box with rococo highlighted in gold. 6″ x 7″ diameter.

Large box, rococo top and bottom. 6½″ square. Newland collection.

Wave Crest box with "blown-out" waves all over top and sides. Dark green. 6¾″ tall x 7½″ diameter. This is one of my most favorite boxes, and cannot really be appreciated from a photo. Brinkman collection.

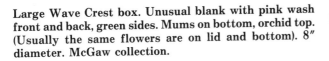

Large Wave Crest box. Unusual blank with pink wash front and back, green sides. Mums on bottom, orchid top. (Usually the same flowers are on lid and bottom). 8″ diameter. McGaw collection.

Classic Wave Crest water scene on top and all 4 sides. Lyle collection.

Large square box with "blown-out" rococo, 7″ square. Newland collection.

Two medium boxes. Left: Unusual blue-lavender shading. Right: Unusual portrait in Wave Crest (usually Nakara). Lyle collection.

Left: Large Wave Crest footed egg crate box. Exceptional design which is equal on all four sides; an unusual feature on Wave Crest pieces, typical Wave Crest green. See Belle Ware section. 6½″ square. Right: Medium egg crate box, 4″ tall x 5″ square.

Large egg crate box with hand-decorated lady and overall beading. 6½″ square. Brinkman collection.

Left: Medium hand-painted egg crate box. Decoration is a fine petit point. This is Wave Crest top of the line, as far as decoration is concerned. Right: Wave Crest box in satin and shiny motif. Gold over shiny is unusual, and has a lovely effect. 4″ tall x 5″ square.

Large and medium footed boxes in a most unusual combination of shiny blue and white. These were purchased separately, and are still the only ones I've seen. Lyle collection.

Large egg crate (or puffy) footed box in unusual light blue color with lillies (also unusual). Lyle collection.

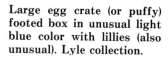

Same as above but with unique Wave Crest gold tracery. The Lyles must have a magnet for blue! Lyle collection.

Left: Glove box, 9½″ x 4½″ wide. Right: Rectangular footed egg crate box in unusual colors. I have a signed Mt. Washington biscuit jar in the identical colors. 6½″L x 4½″W.

Footed glove box, 9½″L x 4½″W.

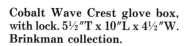

Cobalt Wave Crest glove box, with lock. 5½″T x 10″L x 4½″W. Brinkman collection.

Glove box in ususual combination of pink and yellow. Lyle collection.

Large footed handkerchief box.

Large box with exceptional decoration. Note key. 9¾″ x 7½″. Newland collection.

Large handkerchief with much rococo. Dee's Antiques collection.

Large footed handkerchief box. Well decorated with classic Wave Crest vermillion outline. Andes collection.

Large handkerchief box with cherubs on lid. Lyle collection.

Beautiful large handkerchief box with maiden riding a fish. Gilliam collection.

Lovely Wave Crest box in deep cobalt blue. Same as crystal. 3½″ x 7″ diameter. Brinkman collection.

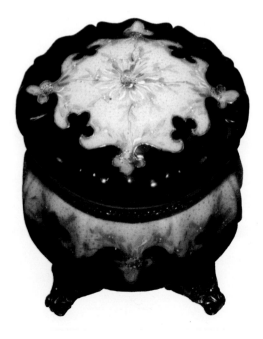

Medium footed box with deep cobalt blue. 5¾″ tall. Brinkman collection.

Lovely large footed box with excellent floral decoration in deep cobalt blue. 6½″ square. Brinkman collection.

Same as above, but with roses. Cobalt finished in shiny decor. Lyle collection.

Left: Beautiful cobalt blue hand-painted large box with courting couple. 8″ diameter. Right: Medium cobalt box with florals. 5½″ diameter.

Unusual heavy painting - almost like frosted look of Belle Ware. Neale-Schlotfeldt collection.

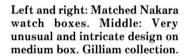

Left and right: Matched Nakara watch boxes. Middle: Very unusual and intricate design on medium box. Gilliam collection.

Footed box with metal base. Shadow effect of background is virtually identical to that used on Mount Washington Opal Ware and Burmese glass. Lyle collection.

Octagon box, more common in Nakara. Lyle collection.

Two large boxes. Beading on right is unusual for Wave Crest. Coutermash collection.

Collars and cuffs. Unusual lid to go with egg crate bottom. Design on lid is unusual. Andes collection.

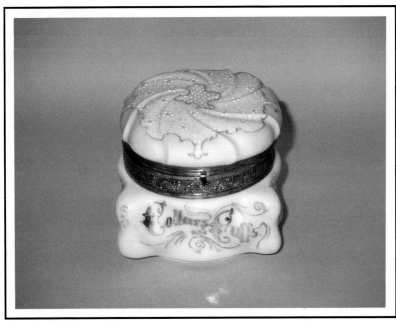

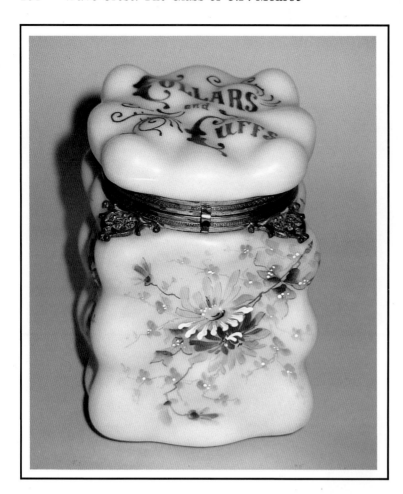

Egg crate collars and cuffs. Andes collection.

Helmschmied Swirl, hinged, biscuit jar with beading. The latter and pastel wash are unusual in Wave Crest. Andes collection.

Left: Footed box with mirror lid. Key lock. The lid may well have been broken and replaced with the mirror. 6″ square. Right: Box with clear bevelled glass in lid, marked "Handkerchiefs". The script and painting look old, and this may be original. 7″ diameter. Newland collection.

Left: Signed with the Wave Crest black mark, but I don't believe it! The blank, metal, and decoration are all Pairpoint. Nothing about it says Wave Crest. Right: Cigar humidor, however I feel the metal has been plated. Also, I truly wonder if Wave Crest ever put a squirrel finial on the lid. William Sprague, Jr. collection.

Wave Crest Trays (Open)

Various trays. Note leaves attached to rim of #3. 4½″ to 5½″ diameter.

Left: Ash receiver with blue interior color, 5″ square. Middle: Very unusual blank, 5½″ long. I feel this may be the tray to the Wave Crest soap dish, which I have never seen. See supplement to 1900-01 catalog. Right: Small tray with two children in sun bonnets. Transfer, 3½″ diameter. Newland collection.

Three footed jewel trays. Probably all three were originally lined, although the one on the left may not have been. Note blue coloring of glass on inside. Footed trays are hard to find. #1. 5″ square; #2. 5″ x 3½″ width; #3. 4¼″ diameter.

Left: Large tray with intricate design and much gold. Right: Same with unusual dark green color and gold stippling or wash. 7″ diameter.

Three trays, left one is footed and cobalt blue. #1. 5½″ diameter; #2. 7″ diameter; #3. 5″ square.

Various ash trays, pin trays, and jewel trays. The latter had linings. 3½" to 4½" diameter.

Top: Medium open tray in rare russet color, 5¼" diameter. Left: Tray with rare dark green color, shiny, 4½" diameter. Middle: Shiny cobalt blue, 4" diameter. Right: Unusual light yellow color, 4". diameter.

Various-shaped pin trays, ash trays, and jewel trays. 3" to 3½" diameter.

Left: Long jewel tray - originally lined (great for pencils), 6″ x 3″. Top right: Pin tray or ash receiver. Bottom right: Probably a pin cushion originally, 3½″ diameter.

Large fernery - originally had metal lining with two ring handles like the round ones. 9¾″ x 7½″.

Wave Crest Wall Plaques

Wall plaque, lovely painting of maiden similar to vase on page 45. 8½" x 12". I have never seen a signed wall plaque.

Wall plaque, with fine painting. Note hearts "carved" on tree trunk. 8" x 10½". CH (Carl Helmschmied), CM (Charles Monroe), VB (unknown)

Wall plaque, a lovely lady surrounded by flowers. 8½″ x 12″. Newland collection.

Wall plaque, exceptional painting of winter snow scene. 5½″ diameter.

Wall plaque, Venetian scene, dark green border. 9¾″ diameter.

Wall plaque, Venetian scene, cobalt blue. 9¾″ diameter.

Wall plaque in gorgeous floral design with exceptional colors in rare and intricate frame. 7″ x 10″.

Wall plaque, winter scene. Note two deer center left. 9¾″ diameter.

Wall plaque, unusual snow scene. Note couple on path in horizon. 8½″ x 12″. Newland collection.

Wall plaque in wooded scene. 7″ x 10″.

Floral wall plaque. 8½″ x 12″.

Wall plaque, unusual blue-grey background. 8½″ x 12″. Newland collection.

Wall plaque, unusual blue background. 7¼″ diameter. Newland collection.

Wall plaque, fern decoration. 9¾″ diameter.

Wall plaque, daisies and clover. 9¾″ diameter. Newland collection.

Wall plaque, floral design. 7¼″ diameter.

Wall plaque, 9¾″ diameter. Newland collection.

Wall plaque, floral design. 7¼″ diameter.

Wall plaque, unusual blank. 7¼″ diameter. Newland collection.

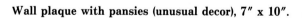

Wall plaque with pansies (unusual decor), 7″ x 10″.

Wall plaque with rural cabin.

Wall plaque with classic Wave Crest scene.

Floral plaque with very dark green background. Andes collection.

Floral plaque with roses. Lyle collection.

Plaque with transfer of Indian. Note different colors on border. Lyle collection.

Nakara plaque with transfer of Queen Louise, rare. Dee's Antiques collection.

Plaque with transfer of deer. Lyle collection.

Plaque with transfer of deer. Neale-Schlotfeldt collection.

Plaque with transfer of lion. Neale-Schlotfeldt collection.

Extremely rare, absolutely magnificent framed picture, painted on glass. Signed "C.F. Monroe, Meriden, Conn." Lyle collection.

Nakara Items

A collection of Nakara ring boxes. These, believe it or not, are rare. They come in florals and portraits, which are all transfers. They never have clips and originally were lined. Note the different shape of the two outside ones with the courting couple. This latter shape is the only one I've seen in Wave Crest. 2″ x 2¼″.

Various open trays, ash trays, etc. Note different washes inside. Pristine lining in center. Right one has unusual maple leaf decor. Strange, broken object in bottom right was bought in Meriden, Connecticut. It supposedly was a throw away from the factory. I thought it was for a regular peg lamp, although I've never seen one. I now feel it was for a smoke set. See page 138.

Left: Footed small bishop's hat mold box, 4¼″ diameter. **Right:** Open bon-bon tray with unusual contrasting colors. 6½″ diameter. Newland collection.

Left: Card holder, hard to find in Nakara. **Middle:** Medium box, 6″ diameter. **Right:** Unusual rectangular puffy tray. This "puffy or egg crate" blank is very rare in anything but Wave Crest. Newland collection.

Top left: Large ash tray, 6″ diameter. Top middle: Hair receiver. Top right: Card holder. Bottom left: Pin receiver (I always thought this was an open salt. It hit me one day when I was looking through the 1895-96 catalog on page 14). 1″ x 2½″. Bottom middle: Rare alcohol lamp. Bottom right: Small ash tray.

From left: Pin tray, pink wash inside; match holder; cracker jar; light pink tray; tray with original lining; rare alcohol lamp (probably used to light smoking materials). 1¼″ x 1¾″.

Top left: Small bishop's hat mold with portrait (transfer), 4½″ diameter. Top right: Small box with Kate Greenway figures, 2¾″ x 4″. Bottom left: Unusual footed match holder. Bottom right: Match holder, 1½″tall x 2½″. Newland collection.

From left: #1. Hexagon box, 3″ x 3¼″; #2. 4-sided "scalloped" box mirror, 2¾″ x 4″; #3. Small round box, 2¼″ x 3¾″ diameter; #4. Footed hexagon box in unusual light blue color.

Left: Blue oval box, 2¾″ x 5¼″. Right: Medium box with cherubs. Transfer. 6″ diameter. Newland collection.

Top left: Blown-out pansy. Top right: Extremely rare blown-out iris. Bottom left and right: Small round boxes with cherubs on lids, transfers. 3¾″ diameter.

Left: Round box with transfer cherub, 2¼″ x 3¾″ diameter. Middle: Footed medium crown mold box with panels of sailing scenes. Hand painted, 6½″ diameter. Right: Footed box with Kate Greenway figures. Transfer. Lining is pristine. 2¾″ x 4″.

Left: Large crown mold, 8½″ diameter. Right: Medium octagon with iris flowers. 6″ diameter.

Left: Mirror in lid, clip missing, 4½″ diameter. Middle: 18th century courting couple. Hard to find peach color, 6″ diameter. Right: Small box. All three are transfers.

Left: Unusual-shaped footed box, 2¾″ x 4″. Middle: Large "Spindrift" box, 8″ diameter. Right: I believe this to be Nakara in a beaded Persian design. It looks a great deal like Webb's work. However, it is Opal Ware and the metal is typical of C.F. Monroe. Metal covers the whole bottom.

From left: #1. Bishop's hat; #2. Bishop's hat, footed with transfer; #3. Bishop's hat, footed, peach color; #4. Unusual shaped footed box in peach color.

Left: Mirror box with cross on lid, clip missing. 5″ diameter. Middle: Mirror box, 4½″ diameter. Right: Footed with cross on lid.

Left: Large box with cherubs, transfer, 8″ diameter. Right: Medium box with Kate Greenway figures. Transfer, 6″ diameter.

Left: Medium bishop's hat blank. This blank is getting increasingly hard to find. 6¾″ diameter. Right: Large round box with no rococo in glass. 8″ diameter.

Large and small bishop's hat boxes. Lyle
collection.

Rectangular box, rare shape for Nakara. Gilliam
collection.

Two medium boxes. Left: Crown mold
with transfer of Niagra Falls. I have seen
two other pieces with this transfer. Right:
Bishop's hat mold. Lyle collection.

Left: Pin holder with B.P.O.E. Middle: Unusual open tray with stag transfer. Right: Match holder. Neale-Schlotfeldt collection.

Left: Unusual box with glass top and entire bottom in metal. All of the others I have seen like this are Kelva. Note "rolled" side at bottom. 3½″ x 5″ overall. Right: Hair receiver with Kate Greenaway figures. Transfer. 2″ x 4¼″. McGaw collection.

Two cigar humidors. Left: Extremely rare owl on tree. Transfer. Right: Geometric design, 5½″ x 4″.

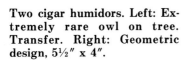

Left: Large cigar humidor with transfer. Bottom is same as biscuit jar blank. 7¾″ x 6½″. Right: Cigar humidor, clip is gone, but does not decrease value as far as I'm concerned. 5½″ x 4″.

Left: Cigar humidor in unusual dark russet color, 5½″ x 4″. Middle: Medium box with courting couple on lid, transfer, 6″ diameter. Right: Tobacco humidor in dark blue.

Left: Large box with metal finial in lid, 4″ x 8″ diameter. Right: Cigar humidor, 5½″ x 4″. Newland collection.

Blue cigar humidor.

B.P.O.E. tobacco (on lid) humidor; match holder. Lyle collection.

Left: A most unusual item. B.P.O.E. humidor with ash receiver (??) for lid. Right: Cigar humidor, note absence of B.P.O.E. Lyle collection.

Tobacco humidor with same unusual lid in silver, but rings on side (same as ferner inserts). Coutermash collection.

Lion humidor (with incorrect lid, I feel), rare. Lyle collection.

Left: Humidor, transfer, "The Old Sport", 7″ tall. Right: Humidor, 5¼″ x 6″. McGaw collection.

Same shape as top photo, but with correct lid. Brenner collection.

Left: Match holder, 2¼″ diameter. Middle: Extremely rare and unusual tobacco humidor, 6″ diameter. Right: Cigar holder, quite rare in Nakara, 2¼″ x 3″. Newland collection.

Very rare smoker's set. Brass fittings. Top is alcohol burner. Middle is match holder. Bottom is ash receiver. Newland collection.

Very rare smoke set. Center for cigars, sides for matches, front for ashes. William Sprague, Jr. collection.

A group of pink Nakara. From left, clockwise: Mirror tray, vase ornament with cherub, medium tray, small tray, hair receiver and match holder.

From left: #1. Unusual match holder, 1½″ x 2″; #2. Extremely rare cruet. Murray's "cruets" has one decorated and signed, 6¼″ x 3¾″. I have also found an identical cruet in satin ruby glass, decorated with pansies, but without the metal handle (maker ??); #3. Peach colored ash tray; #4. Peach mirror tray, 4″ diameter.

Left: Small mirror tray with pastel color inside. Probably never lined. 3¾″ diameter. Right: Medium box with Kate Greenway figures, transfer, 6″ diameter. Newland collection.

Large box with portrait, transfer, 8″ diameter. Newland collection.

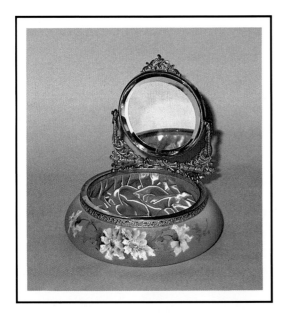

Medium mirror tray, new lining. Lyle collection.

Large box with ladies in Greco-Roman garden, transfer, 8″ diameter. McGaw collection.

Lovely large round box, transfer with signature, "copyright 1907 by Philip Boileau", 8″ diameter. Newland collection.

Left: Lovely large box with finial in lid. The finial is held on with a washer and nut and is for decoration only. 4″ x 8″ diameter. Right: Octagon medium box, 6″ diameter.

Large peach box with much rococo, 3¾″ tall x 7¼″ diameter. Brinkman collection.

Absolutely gorgeous large footed box with goldfish. I'm not sure if this is Wave Crest or Nakara. 8″ diameter. Newland collection.

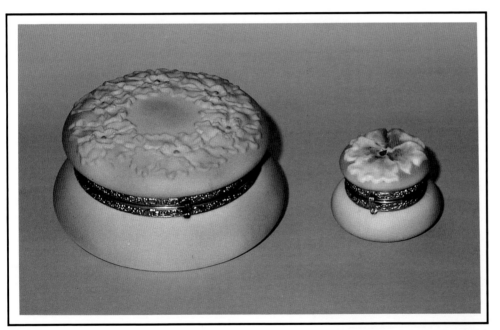

Left: Large blown-out box in an unfinished condition, I feel. Right: Pink blown-out pansy. Lyle collection.

Queen Louise box in rare blue (mostly in green). McGaw collection.

Large footed box in rare burmese coloring. Gilliam collection.

Large bishop's hat box, hand-painted design. Note dancing couple in background. McGaw collection.

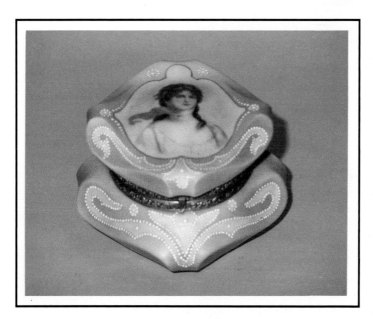

Large bishop's hat box with portrait (transfer) of Queen Louise. Andes collection.

Collars and cuffs. Gilliam collection.

Portrait, collars and cuffs. Gibson girl, transfer. McGaw collection.

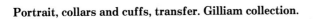

Portrait, collars and cuffs, transfer. Gilliam collection.

Nakara vase in a rare simulated burmese color. Note circular swirls, also unusual for Nakara. Vases of this size are very rare in Nakara. This blank is slightly different from Wave Crest ones of similar sizes. 9″ x 6″.

Same as above, but in green. Gilliam collection.

Three vases of different decoration, but same blank, 8″ tall.

Small vase, in hard to find shape.
Neale-Schlotfeldt collection.

Rare vase in Nakara, green with pink at top. 7½″ x 7½″.

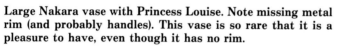

Large Nakara vase with Princess Louise. Note missing metal rim (and probably handles). This vase is so rare that it is a pleasure to have, even though it has no rim.

Extremely rare Nakara vase, signed on glass with unusual metal rim. It sits on a metal platform which is signed C.F.M. Co. 384. 7½″ x 7½″.

A most unusual Nakara (signed) planter, shiny.

Ferneries: right is footed. They are quite rare in my experience (i.e. in Nakara).

Rare jardiniere, and very rare in Nakara. Dee's Antiques collection.

Left: Unusual vase with uncommon foot. 7¾″ tall. Middle: Rare blank, handles are missing from rim. 7¾″ tall. Right: Rare vase with applied ceramic flowers. Unusual brass rim and foot. Signed in metal C.F.M. Co. 490. Left and right are identical blanks. The effect of the hardware creates such a different appearance, I didn't realize it until I looked at the photo.

Left: Large bishop's hat box with applied ceramic flowers. These are quite rare. Transfer is author signed. 5″ x 9″. Right: Large round Nakara box with Princess Louise. I had only seen this in green until one blue one surfaced. 3½″ x 8″ diameter.

Three rare boxes with applied ceramic flowers. Note missing clip on box on right. These boxes have never survived without broken petals, so don't pass on one if offered to you. #1. & #3. 3¼″ x 4½″.

Medium-sized box with bisque flowers. 7″ diameter. Brinkman collection.

Nakara medium-to-large octagon box with applied china flowers. Note different size petals in first two boxes.

Ferner, rare with applied flowers. Dee's Antiques collection.

Left: Rare Indian letter or cigar or pencil holder? Metal. Bottom: This is the blank used for the wall whisk broom holder. 4″ x 4¾″. Right: Indian biscuit jar, signed. This also comes in a handsome russet color instead of green. It also comes with a metal humidor top. 5¼″ x 6″.

Left: Cigarette holder with Indian transfer. 3¼″ x 3½″. Middle: Humidor with Indian transfer. 5¼″ x 6″. Right: Very rare salt and pepper with Indian transfer. 3¾″ overall x 1½″. McGaw collection.

Left: Humidor, rare shape with Indian. Transfer with hand-painted colors. Typical C.F. Monroe. Metal fittings - unsigned. 7½" overall x 4½". Right: Tobacco humidor with "Bill Cody" transfer. I have seen this design and blank made into a biscuit jar. 5¾" x 6½".

Left: Very rare blotter. Right: Indian cigar humidor. Similar to one with scout. 5¾" x 6½". Newland collection.

Rare Nakara umbrella stand. Open at bottom with metal sleeve almost to floor. Indian on one side and scout on horse on opposite side. 20½″ tall overall.

Opposite side of umbrella stand. If top is closed, this becomes a jardiniere stand. See 1900-01 supplement.

Umbrella stand, same as previous one, in different colors. Note different rim. McGaw collection.

Spectacular, large hand-painted vase with Indian, on Opal Ware. All others are transfers. I'm fairly sure this is C.F. Monroe. 11¾″ x 7½″.

Nakara. I have no idea what this unusual piece was used for. It is shown here in two views. The opening must have had a metal collar, and the base had a footed piece. Note the paint dots below the opening with which to affix the plaster. 6½" x 5" x 3¾" high.

Nakara bon-bon in rare peach color. Note paint inside.

Kelva Items

Kelva. Center: Rare biscuit jar in rare peach color. I have never seen another biscuit jar in Kelva. Counter clockwise: Match holder, 1½″ x 2½″; Three napkin rings (also comes in red); Smoke set: match and cigar holder, 2½″ x 2¾″; Salts in different shapes and colors.

Left two: Pair of vases with unusual decor. Beaded pastel ribbons, go around vases, and are Nakara-type painting. Bases of dark shiny green and russet are Wave Crest-type painting, 7¾″ x 2¾″. Middle: Unusual vase (shape also in Wave Crest) in red, 7¼″ x 3″. Right: Rare footed vase in fuscia, 6″ x 2″.

Left: Kelva footed medium crown mold box. Note: Nakara-like beading and pastel color between Kelva panels. Right: Lovely Nakara crown mold box with pastoral scenes. Both 6½" diameter. Newland collection.

Top left: Large box in blue with pastel pink and beading, 3½" x 8". Top right: Very dark green oval box with beading. Color is so dark, Kelva effect didn't show well in photo. 2¾" x 5¼". Bottom left: Small box in blue similar to top left. 3" diameter. Bottom right: Blown-out rose. 3¾" x 2½".

#1. Salt and pepper, 3″ tall. #2. Vase with unusual second color on bottom rococo, 7¾″ tall. McGaw collection.

Left: Small shown here for comparison in size. 3″ x 3¼″. Right: Medium metal box with glass lid. Rare in this size. 5″ diameter. Newland collection.

Ferneries. Left: Fuscia. Right: Red, quite rare, 4¼″ x 7½″.

Large box with roses, 8″ diameter. Newland collection.

Left: Oval box, 2¾″ x 5¼″. Middle: Small hexagon box with beading and pastel colors, 3″ x 3¼″. Right: Metal box with glass lid, 3″ x 3¾″. Front: Rare salt and pepper. Newland collection.

Left: Cigar humidor in rare chocolate brown color, 4¾" x 3½". Middle: Unusual box, only the lid is glass, 3" overall x 3¾". Right: Cigars (written on lid) with pastoral scene with cows. This same appearing blank appears in 1895-96 catalog as condensed milk can holder, but in Wave Crest.

Left: Humidor, "Cigars" on front, 5¼" x 6¼". Right: Box with pastel panels, 6" diameter. Newland collection.

Left: Unusual match holder and ash receiver. Middle: Medium tray. Crown mold, 6¼" diameter. Right: Small handled tray, 3" diameter. Newland collection.

Left: Green open tray. Note a lot of trim on Kelva is silver plated, 6½″ diameter. Right: Kelva green ferner or planter.

Kelva cigar humidor in rare brown color. Script is difficult to see. Philip Gordon collection.

Right: Kelva box with unusual gold painting. Lyle collection.

Blue Kelva cigar humidor. Blue Kelva whisk broom holder. Gilliam collection.

Red Kelva whisk broom holder. Neale-Schlotfeldt collection.

Large green Kelva vase. Lyle collection.

18½″ tall Kelva vase. Note metal is silverplated. Not uncommon on Kelva pieces. Lyle collection.

Blue Kelva vase. St. John collection.

Kelva vase in light green. Shape is similar, but different to Nakara Princess Louise vase. 14″ tall overall.

Unusual Kelva vase in rare dark green (almost black) with Nakara-type shading at top.

Cut Glass*

Cut glass. Left: Large bowl with sterling rim marked C.F.M. Co., 4″ x 9¼″. Jewel box with swivel mirror in lid. Gold leafed rim as metal was tarnished. 3½″ x 4″.

#1. Small round box, pin wheel, 2¾″ x 4″; #2. Medium box, hobstar, 4″ x 6¼″; #3. Small bishop's hat, 3¼″ x 3½″; #4. Small hexagon, 3″ x 3¼″. Many of the cut glass boxes were made in the same mold shape as the Opal Ware boxes. This is without signatures. In this regard I am able to identify makers even when cut glass dealers don't know.

Left: Medium box in crown mold shape. Center of lid comes to a point, but this is difficult to see in photo. See page 158. 3¾″ x 5½″. Right: Medium handkerchief box. 4¼″ x 6¼″.

* The sterling rims of the boxes are signed ''CFM Co. Sterling'' near the hinge if the rim is flat.

Identical cut glass mirror boxes with different sterling silver rims, 3¼″ x 5¾″. Left: Dealer who had this was not sure it was C.F.M. Co. I was positive. My wife, in cleaning it, took mirror out, and the paper backing the mirror had dateline: "1905 Meriden, Conn." Note: mirrors have new aluminum foil under lid. Right: Original puff with new tab.

Left: Small crystal box with unusual colored flowers in non-satin panels. 3″ x 4″. Right: Small cut glass box, 3″ x 4″. Newland collection.

8″ cut glass bowl. Signed C.F.M. Co. in bottom of bowl. Lyle collection.

Large cut glass handkerchief box. 7¾″ square. Andes collection.

Left: Medium cut glass box in bishop's hat design. Right: Cut glass biscuit jar. Lyle collection.

Two cut glass boxes. Right one in octagon design. Lyle collection.

Left: Uncut crystal box. Middle and right: Two small cut glass boxes. Lyle collection.

Cut glass ferner with liner. Lyle collection.

Rare cut glass spindle. Neale-Schlotfeldt collection.

Unusual cut glass box, medium size, with raised center. Lyle collection.

Belle Ware, Handel, and Keystone*

Left: Unusual crystal box in frosted finish with stained glass appearance on lid. Right: Opal box in classical Belle Ware shape. Both top and bottom are fully decorated with flowers, but entirely different in design.

Belle Ware. Box is signed Belle Ware, but could easily be mistaken for Wave Crest, except for shape and signature. The green color, flowers, couple, and especially the vermillion and gold outlines are all very similar to Wave Crest.

Left: Hand-painted opal biscuit jar in "frosted" finish. The granular look comes from tiny glass beads that have been partially melted and fused. This is a classical Belle Ware trait. Right: Opal bowl.

* These last four pages are shown for comparison of other companies' opal ware.

All four opal pieces are signed. The shapes are typical to Belle Ware and and different from Wave Crest. The small jewel box is finished in the frosted technique, 4¼″ x 3″.

All signed Belle Ware. Top: Two small vases with C.V.H. raised in the mold in the bottom, 5¼″ x 2¼″. Bottom: Salts. Three are done in frosted finish. #3, from left, is a rare form in satin finish, 3¾″ tall.

Large vase decorated by C.V. Helmschmied, himself, probably when he owned Belle Ware. Dee's Antiques collection.

Handel. Left: Opal Ware jewel box signed H (in diamond) Meriden Ct. Very similar to Wave Crest. Right: Tobacco humidor in hand-painted Opal Ware signed "Handel Ware" #72/128 Decorated by P.J. Handel Meriden CT. U.S.A.", 5¼″ x 5″.

Keystone Ware: "H.M. RIO Co. Philadelphia, PA." A contemporary of C.F. Monroe. Quite hard to find. All are signed except the small red jewel box. Muffineer is 5″ tall.

Unusual collection of Mount Washington "Dresden" decorated Opal Ware. Box is Mount Washington. Double vase is Smith Bros., 8¼″ x 7¼″. Hair receiver is Wave Crest, in an extremely rare shape. See page 83 for signed piece. 4½″ x 3¼″.

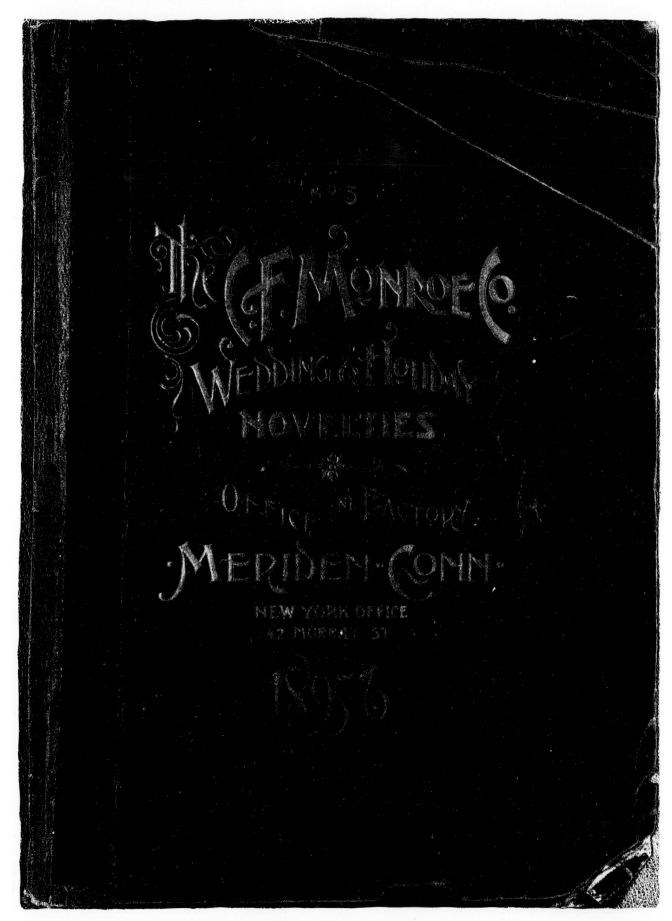

Front cover of the 1895-96 C.F. Monroe catalog.

RICHLY DECORATED CHINA VASE.

This Cut Reduced about one-half from Original Size.

Cupid Vase.

Assortment 5, Decorated, Royal Worcester style, list each,   . $30 00

Assortment 6, Elaborately Decorated, list each,   .   .   50 00

2

From the 1895-96 C.F. Monroe catalog.

RICHLY DECORATED CHINA VASE.

This Cut Reduced about one-half from Original Size.

Dolphin Vase.

Assortment **4**, list each,   .   . $16 00
Assortment **5**, list each,   .   .   20 00

3

From the 1895-96 C.F. Monroe catalog.

DECORATED OPAL FERN DISH AND JARDINIERE.

For Description of Assortments see page 1.

These Cuts Reduced about one-half from Original Size.

WX. Trimming for Fern Dish is Gold Plated, with Perforated Detachable Dish.

Fern Dish 146—WX.

Assortment 4, list each, . $3 00

Jardiniere 185.

Assortment 1,	list each,	.	.	$2 25
Assortment 2,	list each,	.	.	2 50
Assortment 2½,	list each,	.	.	2 70
Assortment 4,	list each,	.	.	6 00
Assortment 5,	list each,	.	.	8 00
Assortment 6,	list each,	.	.	12 00

4

From the 1895-96 C.F. Monroe catalog.

DECORATED OPAL FERN DISH AND JARDINIERE.

For Description of Assortments see page 1.

These Cuts Reduced about one-half from Original Size.

ZX. Trimming with Feet for Fern Dish is Gold Plated with Perforated Detachable Dish.

Fern Dish 146—ZX.

Assortment 5, list each,   . $6 50

Jardiniere 50.

Assortment 1,	list each,	.	.	$1 00
Assortment 2,	list each,	.	.	1 10
Assortment 2½,	list each,	.	.	1 20
Assortment 4,	list each,	.	.	2 50
Assortment 5,	list each,	.	.	4 00

5

From the 1895-96 C.F. Monroe catalog.

DECORATED OPAL WARE.

GENTLEMEN'S

COLLAR AND CUFF

BOX,

TOP ONLY IS

SATIN LINED.

MADE WITHOUT

FEET IN THIS

ASSORTMENT ONLY.

Assortment 4, list each,
$7 00

Collar and Cuff 146—MX.

For Description of Assortments, see page 1.

These Cuts Reduced about one-half from Original Size.

Vase 162

Assortment 4, list each,	.	$2 00
Assortment 5, list each,	.	4 00
Assortment 6, list each,	.	6 00
Assortment 7, list each,	.	10 00

Vase 137

Assortment 4, list each,	.	$8 00
Assortment 5, list each,	.	12 00
Assortment 6, list each,	.	24 00
Assortment 7, list each,	.	36 00

6

From the 1895-96 C.F. Monroe catalog.

BILLOW WARE.
DECORATED OPAL COLLAR AND CUFF BOX, SUITABLE FOR GENTLEMEN.
MOUNTED WITH GOLD PLATED TRIMMINGS, WITH FEET.

The Top only is Satin Lined.   For Description of Assortments see page 1.
These Cuts Reduced about one-half from Original Size.

Collar and Cuff 146—MO.

Assortment 5, list each,	.	.	.	$13 00
Assortment 6, list each,	.	.	.	16 00

DECORATED OPAL CIGAR AND TOBACCO BOX.

Mounted with Gold Plated Trimmings, with receptacle at Top for Dampened Sponge or Cloth. This idea being Admirable for Keeping Tobacco Moist.

Cigar 146—OX.				**Tobacco 147—OX.**		
Assortment 4, list each,	.	$7 00		Assortment 4, list each,	.	$6 00
Assortment 5, list each,	.	11 00		Assortment 5, list each,	.	8 50
Assortment 6, list each,	.	13 50	7	Assortment 6, list each,	.	11 00

From the 1895-96 C.F. Monroe catalog.

BILLOW WARE.

DECORATED OPAL HANDKERCHIEF, JEWEL AND PHOTO RECEIVER,

MOUNTED WITH GOLD PLATED TRIMMINGS. SATIN LINED. SCENTED.

For Description of Assortments see page 1.

These Cuts Reduced about one-half from Original Size.

LX. Gold Plated Trimmings, with Feet and Ornamental Corners.

Photo Receiver 167–LX.

Assortment 5, list each,   . $6 50
Assortment 6, list each,   .   10 00

Photo Receivers not lined.

OX. Gold Plated Trimmings, Ornamental Corners.

Handkerchief 148—OX.			**Jewel 149—OX.**		
Assortment 5, list each.	.	$8 50	Assortment 5, list each,	.	$7 50
Assortment 6, list each,	.	12 00	Assortment 6, list each,	.	10 00

BILLOW WARE.

DECORATED OPAL HANDKERCHIEF, JEWEL AND PHOTO RECEIVER,

MOUNTED WITH GOLD PLATED TRIMMINGS. SATIN LINED. SCENTED.

For Description of Assortments see page 1.
These Cuts Reduced about one-half from Original Size.

Handkerchief 146—NX.

Assortment 5, list each,	. .	$13 00
Assortment 6, list each,	. .	16 00
Assortment 7, list each,	. .	24 00

NX. Gold Plated Trimmings with Feet and
Ornamental Corners.

KX. Gold Plated Trimmings with Ornamental Corners.

Jewel 147—NX.

Assortment 5, list each,	.	$10 50
Assortment 6, list each,	.	12 50
Assortment 7, list each,	.	16 00

9

Photo Receiver 167—KX.

Assortment 4, list each,	. .	$2 50

Photo Receivers not lined.

From the 1895-96 C.F. Monroe catalog.

WAVE CREST WARE.
Patented October 4, 1892.

DECORATED OPAL HANDKERCHIEF AND JEWEL BOXES,

MOUNTED WITH GOLD PLATED TRIMMINGS. SATIN LINED. SCENTED.

For Description of Assortments see page 1.

These Cuts Reduced about one-half from Original Size.

O. Gold Plated Hinged Trimmings.

Jewel Box 152—O.   **Jewel Box 151—O.**

The above Jewels are lined bottoms, only, unless otherwise ordered.

Assortment 4, list, per doz.,	.	$18 00
Assortment 4, full lined top and bottom, list, per doz.,		20 00
Assortment 4, not lined, for bon-bon, list, per doz.,		16 00

Assortment 4, list per doz.,	.	$27 00
Assortment 4, full lined top and bottom, list, per doz.,		30 00
Assortment 4, no lining, for bon-bon, list, per doz.,		24 00

Handkerchief Box 130—O.   **Jewel Box 131—O.**

Assortment 4, list each,	.	$5 50
Assortment 5, list each,	.	6 50
Assortment 6, list each,	.	8 00
Assortment 7, list each,	.	9 50

Assortment 4, list each,	.	$4 50
Assortment 5, list each,	.	5 50
Assortment 6, list each,	.	7 50
Assortment 7, list each,	.	9 00

Handkerchief 130—O. and Jewel 131—O. without lining for Bon-Bons, net, each $0.25 less.

10

From the 1895-96 C.F. Monroe catalog.

DECORATED OPAL PIN TRAY, CANDLESTICK, HANDKERCHIEF AND JEWEL BOXES.

MOUNTED WITH GOLD PLATED TRIMMINGS.

For Description of Assortments see page 1.

These Cuts Reduced about one-half from Original Size.

RX. Gold Plated Feet.

SX. Gold Plated Handle.

Pin Tray 181—RX.

Assortment 4, list each,	.	$2 00
Assortment 5, list each,	.	3 00

Candlestick 181—SX.

Assortment 4, list each,	.	$2 00
Assortment 5, list each,	.	3 00

L. Silver Plated only.

L. Silver Plated only.

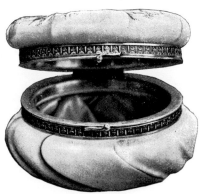

Handkerchief Box 130—L.

Assortment 4, list each,	.	$7 00
Assortment 5 list each,	.	8 00
Assortment 6, list each,	.	9 50
Assortment 7, list each,	.	11 00

Jewel Box 131—L.

Assortment 4, list each,	.	$6 00
Assortment 5, list each,	.	7 00
Assortment 6, list each,	.	9 00
Assortment 7, list each,	.	10 50

Handkerchief 130—L. and Jewel 131—L. without lining for Bon-Bon, net, each $0.25 less.

11

From the 1895-96 C.F. Monroe catalog.

WAVE CREST WARE.

Patented October 4, 1892.

DECORATED OPAL HANDKERCHIEF AND JEWEL BOXES,

MOUNTED WITH GOLD PLATED TRIMMINGS. SATIN LINED. SCENTED.

For Description of Assortments see page 1.

These Cuts Reduced about one-half from Original Size.

O. Trimmings, Gold Plated. L. and NL. Trimmings, Silver Plated Only.

Jewel Box 128—O.

Assortment 4, list each,	.	$5 50
Assortment 5, list each,	.	7 00
Assortment 6, list each,	.	9 00

Handkerchief Box 126—N.

Assortment 4, list each,	.	$8 00
Assortment 5, list each,	.	10 00
Assortment 6, list each.	.	12 50

Handkerchief Box 126—NL.

Assortment 4, list each,	.	$9 50
Assortment 5, list each	.	11 50
Assortment 6, list each,	.	14 00

Jewel Box 128—L.

Assortment 4, list each,	.	$7 00
Assortment 5, list each	,	8 50
Assortment 6, list each,		10 50

12

From the 1895-96 C.F. Monroe catalog.

DECORATED OPAL BON-BON JARS, WITH COVERS LETTERED IN GOLD, "SOUVENIR," AND GOLD PLATED TRIMMINGS, HINGED.

Although Designed for Bon-Bons these can be put to a number of uses.   They are not lined unless so ordered.

Satin lined cover extra, each, $0.20 net.   Full satin lined, top and bottom, extra, each, $0.50 net.

For Description of Assortments see page 1.

These Cuts Reduced about one-half from Original Size.

O. Trimmings, Gold Plated.   L. Trimmings, Silver Plated Only.

12—O.

Assortment 4, not lined, list each,	.	$4 50
Assortment 5, not lined, list each,	.	5 00
Assortment 6, not lined, list each,	.	7 00

121—O.

Assortment 4, not lined, list each,	.	$5 00
Assortment 5, not lined, list each,	.	5 50
Assortment 6, not lined, list each,	.	7 50

46—O.

Assortment 4, not lined, list each,	.	$4 50
Assortment 5, not lined, list each,	.	5 00
Assortment 6, not lined, list each,	.	7 00

46—L.

Assortment 4, not lined, list each,	.	$6 00
Assortment 5, not lined, list each,	.	6 50
Assortment 6, not lined, list each.	.	8 50

13

From the 1895-96 C.F. Monroe catalog.

DECORATED OPAL PUFF, AND GENTLEMEN'S DESK PIN RECEIVER.

These Cuts Reduced about one-half from Original Size.

Pin Receiver 065

Assortment 2, list, per dozen, . $6 00

Puff Box 152—O.

Assortment 4, list per dozen, . $18 00

Assortment 4, without Puffs, net, per dozen, $1.00 less.

DECORATED OPAL TRINKET TRAYS, MOUNTED WITH GOLD TRIMMINGS.

For Description of Assortments see page 1.

These Cuts Reduced about one-half from Original Size.

Trinket Tray 172—O.

Assortment 4, list, per dozen, . $9 00

Trinket Tray 171—O.

Assortment 4, list, per dozen, . $18 00

Trinket Tray 141 O.

Assortment 4, list each,	.	$2 50
Assortment 5, list each,	.	3 50
Assortment 6, list each,	.	5 00

Trinket Tray 142—O.

Assortment 4, list each,	.	$3 00
Assortment 5, list each,	.	4 00
Assortment 6, list each,	.	5 50

Trays not lined, but inside tinted. For Bon-Bons, prices same as above.

14

From the 1895-96 C.F. Monroe catalog.

DECORATED OPAL PUFF BOXES, MOUNTED WITH GOLD PLATED TRIMMINGS.

For Description of Assortments, see page 1.

These Cuts Reduced about one-half from Original Size.

O. Gold Plated Hinged Trimmings.   NX. Gold Plated Hinged Trimings with Feet.

Puff Box 151–O.

| Assortment 4, list each, | . | $2 50 |

Puff Box 131–O.

Assortment 4, list each,	.	$4 50
Assortment 5, list each,	.	5 50
Assortment 6, list each,	.	7 50
Assortment 7, list each,	.	9 00

Puff Box 147—NX.

Assortment 5, list each,	.	$10 50
Assortment 6, list each,	.	12 50
Assortment 7, list each,	.	16 00

Without Puffs, net, each $0.25 less.

Puff Box 128–O.

Assortment 4, list each,	.	$5 50
Assortment 5, list each,	.	7 00
Assortment 6, list each.	.	9 00

15

From the 1895-96 C.F. Monroe catalog.

DECORATED OPAL ATOMIZERS,

MOUNTED WITH NICKEL OR GOLD PLATED TRIMMINGS, NETTED OR PLAIN RUBBER BULBS.

For Netted Bulbs a charge is made of $1.50 more per dozen, net, than for Plain Bulbs.

For Gold Plate a charge is made of $1.50 more per dozen, net, than for Nickel Plate.

These Cuts Reduced about one-half from Original Size.

For Description of Assortments, see page 1.

178 Nickel Top, Plain Bulbs.

Assortment 1, list. per doz. $12 00
Assortment 2, list. per doz. 13 20
Assortment 2½, list. per doz. 13 20

163 Nickel Top, Plain Bulbs.

Assortment 1, list. per doz. $14 40
Assortment 2, list. per doz. 16 00
Assortment 2½, list. per doz. 18 00

156 Nickel Top, Plain Bulbs.

Assortment 2½ list. per doz. $18 00
Assortment 4, list. per doz 27 00
Assortment 5½, list. per doz. 36 00

Assortment 5½ consists of 6 Decorations on Glazed Tinted Ground, Assorted Colors, Traced in Gold.

173 Nickel Top, Netted Bulbs.

Assortment 4, list, per doz., $27 00

166 Nickel Top, Netted Bulbs.

Assortment 4, list, per doz., $36 00
Assortment 5, list, per doz., 42 00

177 Nickel Top, Netted Bulbs.

Assortment 1, Dresden,
list, per doz., $33 00

16

From the 1895-96 C.F. Monroe catalog.

DECORATED OPAL ATOMIZERS,

MOUNTED WITH NICKEL OR GOLD PLATED TRIMMINGS, NETTED OR PLAIN RUBBER BULBS.

For Netted Bulbs a charge is made of $1.50 more per dozen, net, than for Plain Bulbs.
For Gold Plate a charge is made of $1.50 more per dozen, net, than for Nickel Plate.

These Cuts Reduced about one-half from Original Size.

For Description of Assortments, see page 1.

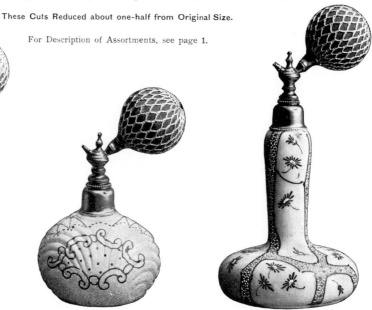

176 Nickel, Netted Bulbs.
Assortment 5, list, per dozen, $36 00

175 Gold, Netted Bulbs.
Assortment 5, list, per dozen, $48 00

174 Gold, Netted Bulbs.
Assortment 5, list, per dozen, $48 00

184 Gold, Netted Bulbs.
Assortment 5, list, per dozen, $54 00
Assortment 6, list, per dozen, 72 00

165 Gold, Netted Bulbs.
Assortment 5, list, per dozen, $54 00
Assortment 6, list, per dozen, 60 00

155 Gold, Netted Bulbs,
Assortment 5, list, per dozen, $48 00
Assortment 6, list, per dozen, 60 00

17

From the 1895-96 C.F. Monroe catalog.

DECORATED OPAL TOILET ARTICLES.

These Cuts Reduced about one-half from Original Size.

Height, 7¼ in.
103 Cologne.

Asst. 4, per doz., list, . . $30 00
Asst. 5, per doz., list, . . 60 00
Asst. 6, per doz., list, . . 90 00

Height, 5¾ in.
102 Cologne.

Asst. 2, Glazed, per doz., list, $7 00
Asst. 2½, Bisque, per doz., list, 7 00

Height, 4½ in.
101 Cologne.

Asst. 2, Glazed, per doz., list, $4 50
Asst. 2½, Bisque, per doz., list, 4 50

Height, 4¾ in.
81 Vase.

Asst 2, Glazed, per doz., list, $3 50
Asst. 2½, Bisque, per doz., list, 4 00

For Description of Assortments see top of page 32.

18

From the 1895-96 C.F. Monroe catalog.

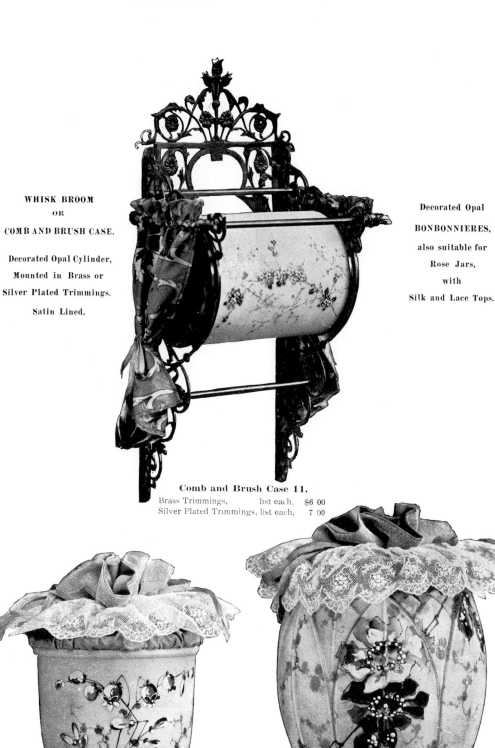

WHISK BROOM
OR
COMB AND BRUSH CASE.

Decorated Opal Cylinder,
Mounted in Brass or
Silver Plated Trimmings.

Satin Lined.

Decorated Opal
BONBONNIERES,
also suitable for
Rose Jars,
with
Silk and Lace Tops.

Comb and Brush Case 11.

Brass Trimmings,	list each,	$6 00
Silver Plated Trimmings, list each,		7 00

Bon-Bon 51.

Assortment 4, list each,	.	$2 00
Assortment 5, list each,	.	2 50

Bon-Bon 135.

Assortment 4, list each,	.	$2 00
Assortment 5, list each,	.	3 00

These Cuts Reduced about one-half from Original Size.

Assortment 4 are Bisque Finish, Assorted Tints and Decorations.
Assortment 5 are Bisque Finish, Assorted Tints and Decorations, Traced in Gold.

19

From the 1895-96 C.F. Monroe catalog.

DECORATED OPAL BONBONNIERES, WITH SILK AND LACE TOPS.

ALSO SUITABLE FOR ROSE JARS.

These Cuts Reduced about one-half from Original Size.

Bon-Bon 128.

Assortment 4, list each,	.	$3 00
Assortment 5, list each,	.	3 50

Bon-Bon 12.

Assortment 2½, list each,	.	$1 50
Assortment 4, list each,	.	2 00
Assortment 5, list each,	.	3 00

Bon-Bon 46.

Assortment 4, list each,	.	$2 00
Assortment 5, list each,	.	3 00

Bon-Bon 121.

Assortment 4, list each,	.	$3 00
Assortment 5, list each,	.	3 50

Assortment 2½,	Fire Bisque Finish, Assorted Tints and Decorations.
Assortment 4,	Bisque Finish, Assorted Tints and Decorations.
Assortment 5,	Bisque Finish, Assorted Tints and Decorations, Traced in Gold.

20

From the 1895-96 C.F. Monroe catalog.

DECORATED OPAL SYRUPS AND SUGAR SIFTER, MOUNTED WITH SILVER PLATED TRIMMINGS.

For Description of Assortments see page 1.

These Cuts Reduced about one-half from Original Size.

D. Silver Plated Syrup Top, with Lid.

DD. Silver Plated Double Screw Sugar Top.

Syrup 123—D.

Assortment 4, list each,	.	$3 50
Assortment 5, list each,	.	4 50
Assortment 6, list each,	.	6 00

Sugar Sifter 53—DD.

Assortment 1, list each,	.	$0 70
Assortment 3, list each,	.	0 75
Assortment 4, list each,	.	0 92
Assortment 5, list each,	.	1 50

UX. and DX. Silver Plated Syrup Tops, with Lid.

Syrup 53—UX.

Assortment 1, list each,	.	$1 80
Assortment 3, list each,	.	2 00
Assortment 4, list each,	.	2 00
Assortment 5, list each,	.	3 00

Syrup 123—DX.

Assortment 4, list each,	.	$3 50
Assortment 5, list each,	.	4 50
Assortment 6, list each,	.	6 00

21

From the 1895-96 C.F. Monroe catalog.

DECORATED OPAL SUGARS AND CREAMS, MOUNTED WITH SILVER PLATED TRIMMINGS.

These Cuts Reduced about one-half from Original Size.

Sugar 138—Y.

Cream 139—Y.

Sugar and Cream Set, 138 and 139 Y.

Assortment 4, list, per set,	.	$5 50
Assortment 5, list, per set,		7 00

Spoon 161—Y.

Assortment 4, list each,	.	$2 70
Assortment 5, list each,	.	3 50

Sugar 138—YX.

Cream 139—YX.

Sugar and Cream Set, 138 and 139—Y X.

Assortment 4, list, per set,	.	$6 70
Assortment 5, list, per set,	.	8 20

138 and 139 Y X Trimmings, Gold Plated, list per set, $3 00 extra. Description of Assortments see bottom next page.

22

From the 1895-96 C.F. Monroe catalog.

WAVE CREST WARE.
Patented October 4, 1892.

DECORATED OPAL SUGARS AND CREAMS, MOUNTED WITH SILVER PLATED TRIMMINGS.

These Cuts Reduced about one-half from Original Size.

Sugar 122—B.   Cream 123—B.

Sugar and Cream Set, 122 and 123—B.

Assortment 4, list, per set,	.	$6 50
Assortment 5, list, per set,	.	7 50
Assortment 6, list, per set,	.	10 00

Sugar 122—BX.   Cream 123—BX.

Sugar and Cream Set, 122 and 123—B X.

Assortment 4, list, per set,	.	$8 50
Assortment 5, list, per set,	.	9 50
Assortment 6, list, per set,	.	12 00

Assortment 4 are Bisque Finish, Assorted Tints and Decorations.
Assortment 5 are Bisque Finish, Assorted Tints and Decorations, Traced in Gold.
Assortment 6 are Bisque Finish, Assorted Tints and Decorations, Traced in Gold, more elaborate.

23

From the 1895-96 C.F. Monroe catalog.

WAVE CREST WARE.
Patented October 4, 1892.

DECORATED OPAL BODIES, MOUNTED WITH SILVER PLATED TRIMMINGS.

Sugar Sifter 123—C.

Assortment 4, list each,	.	$2 00
Assortment 5, list each,	.	2 68
Assortment 6, list each,	.	4 00

These Cuts Reduced about one-half from Original Size.

For Description of Assortments see page 23.

Decorations on Sugar Sifters and Spoons to match Assortments in 122 and 123 Sugar and Cream Sets.

Condensed Milk Can Holder 170—VX.

Assortment 4, list each,	.	$5 50
Assortment 5, list each,	.	6 50

Spoon Holder 123—A.

Assortment 4, list each,	.	$3 50
Assortment 5, list each,	.	4 00
Assortment 6, list each,	.	5 50

Spoon Holder 125—A.

Assortment 4, list each,	.	$3 50
Assortment 5, list each,	.	4 00
Assortment 6, list each,	.	5 50

Spoon Holder 125—AX.

Assortment 4, list each,	.	$3 50
Assortment 5, list each,	.	4 00
Assortment 6, list each,	.	5 50

24

From the 1895-96 C.F. Monroe catalog.

DECORATED OPAL CRACKER JARS.   SILVER PLATED TRIMMINGS.

The first number denotes shape or article, the letters, style of trimmings, and the following numbers the assortment of decoration.

These Cut Reduced about one-half from Original Size.

DESCRIPTION—Assortment 4, Bisque Finish, Assorted Tints and Decorations.
Assortment 5, Bisque Finish, Assorted Tints and Decorations, Traced in Gold.
Assortment 6, Bisque Finish, Assorted Tints and Decorations, Traced in Gold, more elaborate.

IX. Silver Plated Cover

with Bail.

147—IX.

Assortment 4, list each,	.	$6 50
Assortment 5, list each,	.	9 00
Assortment 6, list each,	.	12 00

150—IX.

Assortment 4, list each,	.	$6 50
Assortment 5, list each,	.	9 00
Assortment 6, list each,	.	12 00

**EO. Silver Plated Trimmings with
Bail Handle.**

**EX. Silver Plated Trimmings, Rococo Scroll
Cover and Shot Bail.**

147—EO.

Assortment 4, list each,	.	$6 50
Assortment 5, list each,	.	9 00
Assortment 6, list each,	.	12 00

25

150—EX.

Assortment 4, list each,	.	$6 50
Assortment 5, list each,	.	9 00
Assortment 6, list each,	.	12 00

From the 1895-96 C.F. Monroe catalog.

DECORATED OPAL CRACKER JARS.   SILVER PLATED TRIMMINGS.

For Description of Assortments, see page 32.

The first number denotes shape of article, the letters style of trimming,
and the following numbers the assortment of decorations.

These Cuts Reduced about one-half from Original Size.

H. Silver Plated
Cover.
Chased Band.

GO.
Silver Plated Cover,
with Bail.

GX. Silver Plated
Cover and Bail.
Made for a Cheap
Jar only.

12—H.

Assortment 4, list each,	.	$2 50
Assortment 5, list each,	.	3 00

12—GO.

Assortment 2½, list each,	.	$3 35
Assortment 4, list each,	.	3 50
Assortment 5, list each,	.	4 00

135—GX.

Assortment 4, list each,	.	$2 50

26

12—GX.

Assortment 2, list each,	.	$2 00
Assortment 2½, list each,	.	2 25

From the 1895-96 C.F. Monroe catalog.

DECORATED OPAL CRACKER JARS.   SILVER PLATED TRIMMINGS.

These Cuts Reduced about one-half from Original Size.

DESCRIPTION—Assortment 4 are Bisque Finish, Assorted Tints and Decorations.
Assortment 5 are Bisque Finish, Assorted Tints and Decorations, Traced in Gold.

H. Silver Plated Cover, Chased Band.   G. Satin Finish Silver Plated Cover, with Bail.

135—H.

Assortment 4, list each,	$2 50
Assortment 5, list each,	3 50

E. Silver Plated Trimmings,
Rococo Cover and Bail.

135—G.

Assortment 4, list each,	$4 00
Assortment 5, list each,	4 50

H. Silver Plated Cover,
Chased Band.

135—E.

Assortment 4, list each,	$5 50
Assortment 5, list each,	6 00

46—H.

Assortment 4, list each,	$2 50
Assortment 5, list each,	3 50

27

From the 1895-96 C.F. Monroe catalog.

DECORATED OPAL CRACKER JARS.   SILVER PLATED TRIMMINGS.

These Cuts Reduced about one-half from Original Size.

DESCRIPTION—Assortment 4 are Bisque Finish, Assorted Tints and Decorations.
Assortment 5 are Bisque Finish, Assorted Tints and Decorations, Traced in Gold.

E. Silver Plated Trimmings, Rococo
Cover and Bail.

46—E

Assortment 4, list each,	.	.	$5 50
Assortment 5, list each,	.	.	6 00

G. Satin Finish Silver Plated Cover,
with Bail.

46—G

Assortment 4, list each,	.	.	$4 00
Assortment 5, list each,	.	.	4 50

EO. Silver Plated Trimmings
with Bail Handle.

46—EO.

Assortment 4, list each,	.	.	$5 50
Assortment 5, list each,	.	.	6 00

H. Silver Plated Cover,
Chased Band.

121—H.

Assortment 4, list each,	.	.	$3 00
Assortment 5, list each,	.	.	4 50

28

From the 1895-96 C.F. Monroe catalog.

WAVE CREST WARE.
Patented October 4, 1892.

DECORATED OPAL CRACKER JARS.   SILVER PLATED TRIMMINGS.

These Cuts Reduced about one-half from Original Size.

DESCRIPTION—Assortment 4, Bisque Finish, Assorted Tints and Decorations.
Assortment 5, Bisque Finish, Assorted Tints and Decorations, Traced in Gold.
Assortment 6, Bisque Finish, Assorted Tints and Decorations, Traced in Gold, more elaborate.

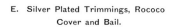

E.   Silver Plated Trimmings, Rococo
Cover and Bail.

121—E.

Assortment 4, list each,			$6 00
Assortment 5, list each,			8 00
Assortment 6, list each,			10 00

128—E.

Assortment 4, list each,			$6 00
Assortment 5, list each,			8 00
Assortment 6, list each,			10 00

EO.   Silver Plated Trimmings
with Bail Handle.

EX.   Silver Plated Trimmings, Rococo
Scroll Cover, and Shot Bail.

128—EO.

Assortment 4, list each,			$6 00
Assortment 5, list each,			8 00
Assortment 6, list each,			10 00

29

121—EX.

Assortment 4, list each,			$6 00
Assortment 5, list each,			8 00
Assortment 6, list each,			10 00

From the 1895-96 C.F. Monroe catalog.

DECORATED OPAL AND CRYSTAL GLASS PITCHERS AND TUMBLERS.

These Cuts Reduced about one-half from Original Size.

For Description of Assortments, see top of page 32. When ordering in sets, which consist of 1 Pitcher and 6 Tumblers, state number of Tumbler and Assortment.

45. Blown Tumbler.

To match 44 Water Bottle.

Asst. 2,	per dozen, list,	$6 00
Asst. 2½,	per dozen, list,	6 50
Asst. 4,	per dozen, list,	12 00
Asst. 5,	per dozen, list,	18 00

44. Water Bottle.

Asst. 2,	per dozen, list,	.	.	$10 00
Asst. 2½,	per dozen, list,	.	.	12 00
Asst. 4,	per dozen, list,	.	.	24 00
Asst. 5,	per dozen, list,	.	.	36 00

Same shape in Pressed Glass called 105, will be $0 40 per dozen less for each Assortment.

Thin Blown Tumbler.

Asst. 1,	per dozen, list,	$5 00
Asst. 2,	per dozen, list,	6 00
Asst. 2½,	per dozen, list,	6 50
Asst. 4,	per dozen, list,	20 00
Asst. 5,	per dozen, list,	36 00

47. Pitcher.

Asst. 1,	per dozen, list,	.	.	$18 00
Asst. 2,	per dozen, list,	.	.	21 60
Asst. 2½,	per dozen, list,	.	.	24 00
Asst. 4,	per dozen, list,	.	.	42 00
Asst. 5,	per dozen, list,	.	.	72 00

30

From the 1895-96 C.F. Monroe catalog.

OPAL SUGARS AND CREAMS.

These Cuts Reduced about one-half from Original Size.

Assorted Decorations and Tints, Nickel Plated Trimmings, Neatly Boxed in Sets.

138 Sugar and 139 Cream.

Assortment 2,	Glazed, Tinted. per dozen sets, list,	.	.	.	$8 00
Assortment 2½,	Bisque Finish, Tinted, per dozen sets, list,	.	.	9 00

DECORATED OPAL SUGAR SIFTERS AND SYRUPS.

Cuts Below, Reduced about one-third from Original Size.

For Description of Assortments see top of page 32.

Sugar Tops. AA. Nickel.   Syrup Tops. S. Nickel.

Pickle Jar.
H. Bright Silver Plated
Cover, Chased Band.

53—AA.   **100—S.**   **74—H. Pickle Jar.**

Asst. 1,	per dozen, list,	$3 00	Asst. 1,	per dozen, list,	$4 00	Asst. 1,	per dozen, list,	$18 00
Asst. 2,	per dozen, list,	3 50	Asst. 2,	per dozen, list,	4 50	Asst. 4.	per dozen, list,	24 00
Asst. 2½,	per dozen, list,	4 00	Asst. 2½.	per dozen, list,	5 00			

31

From the 1895-96 C.F. Monroe catalog.

OPAL SALTS AND PEPPERS, DECORATED, IN 6 DIFFERENT ASSORTMENTS.

The following Salt Cuts Reduced about one-third from the Originals.

DESCRIPTION OF ASSORTMENTS.

Asst 1 consists of 6 Decorations on White Ground, Glazed.
Asst 2 consists of 6 Decorations on Tinted Ground, Glazed.
Asst 2½ consists of 6 Dec. on Tinted Ground, Bisque Finish, same Designs as 2 Asst

Asst. 3 consists of 6 Decorations on Tinted Ground, Glazed, Designs more elaborate.
Asst 4 consists of 6 Dec. on Tinted Ground, Bisque Finish, same Designs as 3 Asst.
Asst. 5 consists of 6 Dec. on Tinted Ground, Bisque Finish, Des. more elaborate with Gold.

67—AA.

Asst. 1,	per gro. list,	$14 00
Asst. 2,	per gro. list,	15 00
Asst 2½,	per gro. list,	18 00

67—BB.

Asst. 1,	per gro. list,	$18 00
Asst. 2,	per gro. list,	19 00
Asst. 2½,	per gro. list,	24 00
Asst. 4.	per gro. list,	30 00
Asst. 5,	per gro. list,	42 00

67—CC.

Asst. 1,	per gro. list,	$24 00
Asst. 2,	per gro. list,	25 00
Asst. 2½,	per gro. list,	27 00
Asst. 4.	per gro. list,	33 00
Asst. 5,	per gro. list,	45 00

68—AA.

Asst. 1,	per gro. list	$14 00
Asst. 2.	per gro. list,	15 00
Asst 2½.	per gro. list,	18 00

68—BB.

Asst. 1,	per gro. list,	$18 00
Asst. 2,	per gro. list,	19 00
Asst. 2½,	per gro. list,	24 00
Asst. 4.	per gro. list,	30 00
Asst. 5,	per gro. list,	42 00

68—CC.

Asst. 1,	per gro. list,	$24 00
Asst. 2,	per gro. list,	25 00
Asst. 2½,	per gro. list,	27 00
Asst. 4.	per gro. list,	33 00
Asst. 5,	per gro. list,	45 00

69—AA.

Asst. 1,	per gro. list,	$14 00
Asst. 2,	per gro. list,	15 00
Asst 2½,	per gro. list,	18 00

69—CC.

Asst. 1,	per gro. list,	$24 00
Asst. 2,	per gro. list,	25 00
Asst. 2½,	per gro. list,	27 00
Asst. 3,	per gro. list,	30 00
Asst. 4.	per gro. list,	33 00

70—AA.

Asst. 1,	per gro. list,	$14 00
Asst. 2,	per gro. list,	15 00
Asst 2½.	per gro. list,	18 00

70—BB.

Asst. 1,		$18 00
Asst. 2,		19 00
Asst. 2½,		24 00

70—CC.

Asst. 1,	per gro. list,	$24 00
Asst. 2.	per gro. list,	25 00
Asst. 2½,	per gro. list,	27 00

72—AA.

Asst. 1,	per gro. list,	$14 00
Asst. 2,	per gro. list,	15 00
Asst. 2½,	per gro. list,	18 00

72—BB.

Asst. 1,	per gro. list,	$18 00
Asst. 2,	per gro. list,	19 00
Asst. 2½,	per gro. list,	24 00
Asst. 3,	per gro. list,	27 00
Asst. 4.	per gro. list,	30 00

73—AA.

Asst. 1,	per gro. list	$14 00
Asst. 2,	per gro. list,	15 00
Asst. 2½,	per gro. list,	18 00

73—BB.

Asst. 1,	per gro. list,	$18 00
Asst 2,	per gro. list,	19 00
Asst. 2½,	per gro. list,	24 00
Asst. 3,	per gro. list,	27 00
Asst. 4.	per gro. list,	30 00
Asst. 5,	per gro. list,	42 00

32

From the 1895-96 C.F. Monroe catalog.

OPAL SALTS AND PEPPERS, DECORATED IN 6 ASSORTMENTS, 6 DECORATIONS IN EACH ASSORTMENT.

The first number designates the shape of article, the letters the style of cap, and the next number the assortment of decorations.

**AA is a Nickel Plate Cap, Single Screw.   BB Silver Plate Cap, Single Screw.
CC Silver Plate Cap, Double Screw.**

73—CC.	96—AA.	96—BB.	96—CC.	97—AA.
Asst. 1, per gro. list, $24 00	Asst. 1, per gro list $14 00	Asst. 1, per gro. list, $18 00	Asst. 1, per gro. list, $24 00	Asst. 1, per gro. list $14 00
Asst. 2, per gro. list, 25 00	Asst. 2, per gro. list, 15 00	Asst. 2, per gro. list, 19 00	Asst. 2, per gro. list, 25 00	Asst. 2, per gro. list, 15 00
Asst. 2½, per gro. list, 27 00	Asst. 2½, per gro. list, 18 00	Asst. 2½, per gro. list, 24 00	Asst. 2½, per gro. list, 27 00	Asst. 2½, per gro. list, 18 00
Asst. 3, per gro. list, 30 00				
Asst. 4, per gro. list, 33 00				
Asst. 5, per gro. list, 45 00				

97—BB.	98—AA.	98—BB.	98—CC.	79—DD.
Asst. 1, per gro. list, $18 00	Asst. 1, per gro. list, $14 00	Asst. 1, per gro. list, $18 00	Asst. 1, per gro. list, $24 00	Asst. 1, per gro. list, $28 00
Asst. 2, per gro. list, 19 00	Asst. 2, per gro. list, 15 00	Asst. 2, per gro. list, 19 00	Asst. 2, per gro. list, 25 00	Asst. 2, per gro. l st, 30 00
Asst. 2½, per gro. list, 24 00	Asst. 2½, per gro. list, 18 00	Asst. 2½, per gro. list, 24 00	Asst. 2½, per gro. list, 27 00	Asst. 2½, per gro. list, 33 00
Asst. 4, per gro. list, 30 00		Asst. 4, per gro. list, 30 00	Asst. 4, per gro. list, 33 00	Asst. 3, per gro. list, 36 00
		Asst. 5, per gro. list, 42 00	Asst. 5, per gro. list, 45 00	Asst. 4, per gro. list 39 00
				Asst. 5, per gro. list, 48 00

HH Nickel Top.   Mustards.   II Silver Plate Top.

80—DD.	79—HH.	79—II.	80—HH.	80—II.
Asst. 1, per gro. list, $28 00	Asst. 1, per gro. list, $19 00	Asst. 1, per gro. list, $30 00	Asst. 1, per gro. list, $19 00	Asst. 1, per gro. list, $30 00
Asst. 2, per gro. list, 30 00	Asst. 2, per gro. list, 20 00	Asst. 2, per gro. list, 32 00	Asst. 2, per gro. list, 20 00	Asst. 2, per gro. list, 32 00
Asst. 2½, per gro. list, 33 00	Asst. 2½, per gro. list, 23 00	Asst. 2½, per gro. list, 36 00	Asst. 2½, per gro. list, 23 00	Asst. 2½, per gro. list, 36 00
Asst. 3, per gro. list, 36 00		Asst. 3, per gro. list, 39 00		Asst. 3, per gro. list, 39 00
Asst. 4, per gro. list, 39 00		Asst. 4, per gro. list, 42 00		Asst. 4, per gro. list, 42 00
Asst. 5, per gro. list, 48 00		Asst. 5, per gro. list, 54 00		Asst. 5, per gro. list, 54 00

From the 1895-96 C.F. Monroe catalog.

"Daisy" Salt.

Patented June 2, 1891.
**FF Silver Plate Top,
Single Screw.**

64—FF.

Asst. 2½, per gro. list, $30 00

"Wave Crest" Salt.

Patented Oct. 4, 1892.
**EE Silver Plate Top,
Double Screw.**

129—EE.

Asst. 4,	per gro. list,	$54 00
Asst. 5,	per gro. list,	78 00
Asst. 6,	per gro. list,	102 00

Billow Salt.

**EE Silver Plate Top,
Double Screw,**

153—EE.

Asst. 4,	per gro. list,	$54 00
Asst. 5,	per gro. list,	78 00
Asst. 6,	per gro. iist,	102 00

Salt.

**GG Silver Plate Top,
Single Screw.**

71—GG.

Asst. 1,	per gro. list,	$18 00
Asst. 2,	per gro. list,	21 00

Decorated Opal Finger Bowl.

99. Tooth Pick.

Asst. 1,	per gro. list,	$13 00
Asst. 2,	per gro. list,	14 00
Asst. 2½,	per gro. list,	16 50
Asst. 3	per gro. list,	30 00
Asst. 4,	per gro. list,	36 00
Asst. 5,	per gro. list,	42 00

Asst. 1, White, Glazed, Gold Edge, per dozen, list,	$4 50
Asst. 2½, Bisque, Assorted Tints and Decorations, per dozen, list.,	5 00
Asst. 5, Bisque, Assorted Tints and Decorations, traced in Gold, per dozen, list,	18 00

76. Open Salt.

Asst. 4,	per gro. list,	$30 00
Asst. 5,	per gro. list,	42 00

65. Open Salt.

Asst. 4,	per gro. list,	$30 00
Asst. 5,	per gro. list,	42 00

Boxes for Salts, 2 in a box, Satin Lined, per doz., list, $1.70.

Napkin Rings.

Detachable Glass Bodies, Nickel Trimmings.

Patented July 6, 1886.

77.

Asst. 1,	per gro. list,	$27 00
Asst. 2,	per gro. list,	30 00
Asst. 2½,	per gro. list,	30 00

Boxes, Satin Lined, 2 in a box, extra per dozen, list, $1 25

Opal Match Safes.

METAL TRIMMINGS.

6. Match Safe.

Asst. 2,	Brass Trimmings, per dozen, list,	$4 50
Asst. 2⅙,	Brass Trimmings, per dozen, list,	7 00
Asst. 2½,	Silver Trimmings, per dozen, list,	8 00

34

From the 1895-96 C.F. Monroe catalog.

BOUDOIR LAMPS.

Richly Decorated Opal Bodies, Mounted
in Gold or Silver Plated Trimmings.

Complete with 8 Inch Shade, Chimney,
Tripod, Argand Burner, Detachable Fount.

Heights from Base to top of Chimney,
18½ and 16 Inches.

These Lamps are desirable
as a novelty, and not only
ornamental, but practical
and useful. They are
smaller than the ordinary
stand or table lamp, but
give the light necessary
to read or sew by, and
make a beautiful gift.

46—U.

| Assortment 4, list each, | $6 70 |
| Assortment 5, list each, | 8 00 |

12—W.

| Assortment 4, list each, | . | . | $6 70 |
| Assortment 5, list each, | . | . | 8 00 |

12—V.

| Assortment 4, list each, | . | . | $6 70 |
| Assortment 5, list each, | . | . | 8 00 |

35

From the 1895-96 C.F. Monroe catalog.

DECORATED OPAL LAMP SHADES AND GLOBES.
FOR PRICES, SEE PAGE 39.

6 Inch Decorated Opal Dome.

10 Inch Decorated Opal Dome.

Decorated Opal Globe.

7 Inch Vienna Decorated Opal Dome.

10 Inch Decorated Opal Melon Dome.

36

From the 1895-96 C.F. Monroe catalog.

DECORATED OPAL LAMP FOUNTS, CAPPED, AND 14 INCH DOMES.

No. 30 Fount.

Fits Holmes, Booth & Haydens' and
E. Miller & Co.'s Fixtures.

No. 32 Fount.

Fits B. & H. and C. Parker Co.'s Fixtures.

No. 52 Fount.

Fits B. & H. and C. Parker Co.'s Fixtures.

14 Inch Decorated Opal Dome.

14 Inch Domes.		**Lamp Founts.**	
Asst. 4990, Glazed, White, Asst. Dec., per doz., list,	$9 50	Asst. 4990, Glazed, White Ground, Asst. Dec., per doz., list,	$4 75
Asst. 4980, Glazed, Tinted, Asst. Dec., per doz., list,	11 50	Asst. 4980, Glazed, Tinted Ground, Asst. Dec., per doz., list,	5 00
Asst. 4960, Bisque, Tinted. Asst. Dec., per doz., list,	13 00	Asst. 4960, Bisque, Tinted Ground, Asst. Dec., per doz., list,	5 50

37

From the 1895-96 C.F. Monroe catalog.

Front cover of the 1899-1900 C.F. Monroe catalog.

DISCOUNT SHEET.

On Orders amounting to less than $100.00, Net,

40 per cent. from List.

On Orders amounting to $100.00 or over, Net,

50 per cent. from List.

TERMS: **2** PER CENT. FOR CASH, **10 DAYS**, NET 30 DAYS.

A NOMINAL CHARGE FOR PACKAGES.

Wave Crest Ware.

Most all the principal Jobbers carry our line; if yours does not, send direct to us.   If unacquainted with our goods, we will cheerfully submit a few samples for inspection, if not satisfactory, to be returned to us within two days from receipt of same with no expense to you; otherwise, to be considered sold.

Reference accompanying first order oftentimes saves delay.

ADDRESS,

THE C. F. MONROE COMPANY,

MERIDEN, CONN.

MANUFACTURERS OF

Wedding and Holiday Novelties.

NEW YORK SALESROOM: 28 BARCLAY STREET.

Discount sheet from the 1899-1900 C.F. Monroe catalog.

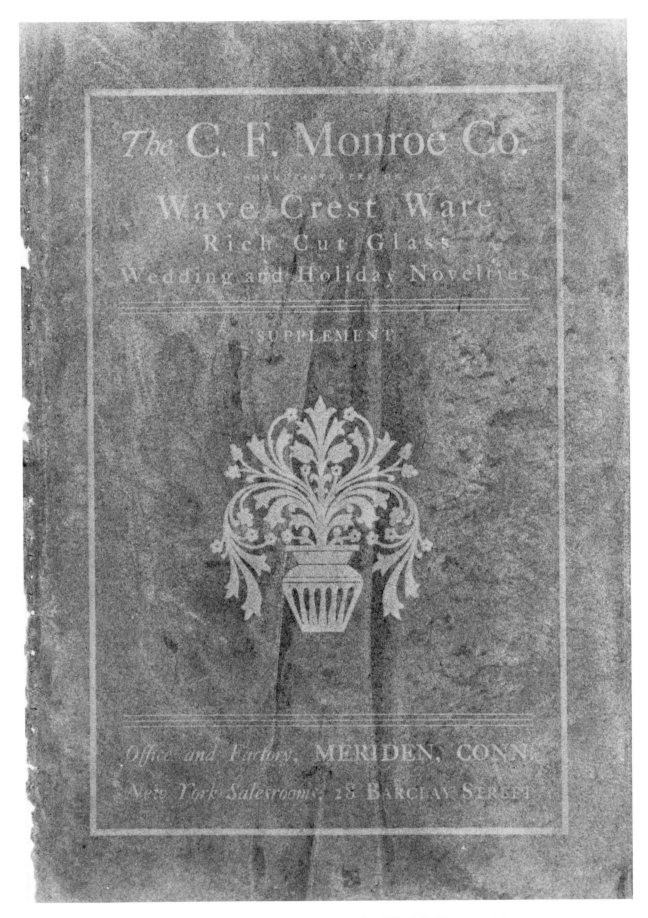

Front cover of the 1901 supplement to the 1900 C.F. Monroe catalog.

1901.

Supplement to Catalogue number 6, 1900,
mailed you last Fall, of

Wave Crest Ware

The cuts, herein, illustrate new goods and changes in our line, which, added to those shown in catalogue you already have, make a most complete and varied assortment.

Our Vase Line this year is especially attractive. The Bud Vases are proving fine sellers, as well as the Ash Trays, and the latter really quite a novelty owing to the manner in which they are mounted. We think there will be no mistake made in ordering any of these or other goods shown here.

RICH CUT GLASS.

Our Cut Glass Line is such that it requires a complete and separate Catalogue to illustrate the different articles we manufacture, but this being a Supplement only to our Wave Crest Ware, we can include only a limited number of cuts in this issue. The name of our house, we believe, will be of sufficient guarantee that the Monroe Cut Glass is of the highest order.

THE C. F. MONROE CO.

MANUFACTURERS OF

RICH CUT GLASS,

WEDDING AND HOLIDAY NOVELTIES.

NEW YORK SALESROOMS: 28 BARCLAY STREET, U. S. A.

MAIN OFFICE AND FACTORIES: MERIDEN, CONNECTICUT, U. S. A.

From the 1901 supplement.

The 1901 supplement to the Monroe catalogue has been reprinted with the permission of the Rakow Library of the Corning Museum of Glass.

INTERIOR VIEW OF THE C. F. MONROE CO.'S NEW YORK STORE, 28 BARCLAY STREET

From the 1901 supplement.

WAVE CREST WARE.

This Jardiniere and Umbrella Stand makes a most attractive and useful piece of furniture. Rich decorations, embossed panels, metal top of artistic design.

These cuts about one-third of original size.

Umbrella Stand without feet, list each $2.00 less for either assortment.

Jardiniere Stand 266 V L.		Umbrella Stand 266—W L.	
Assortment 1, list each, . $19 00	Assortment 4, list each, . $30 00	Assortment 1, list each, . $21 00	Assortment 4, list each, . $32 00
Assortment 2½, list each, . 20 00	Assortment 5, list each, 35 00	Assortment 2½, list each, . 22 00	Assortment 5, list each, . 37 00

From the 1901 supplement.

The 1901 supplement to the Monroe catalogue has been reprinted with the permission of the Rakow Library of the Corning Museum of Glass.

WAVE CREST WARE.

This Jardiniere Stand, with its elaborately embossed and beautifully decorated panels, makes a most ornamental and useful piece of furniture.   The top is of metal, artistic in design and finish.

This cut about one-third of original size.

See Catalogue 6 for prices of Jardinieres to match Stands.

Jardiniere Stand 266—T L.

| Without Jardiniere, Assortment 1, list each, . | . | $16 00 | Without Jardiniere, Assortment 4, list each. . | . | $27 00 |
| Without Jardiniere, Assortment 2½, list each, . | . | 17 00 | Without Jardiniere, Assortment 5, list each. . | . | 32 00 |

3

From the 1901 supplement.

The 1901 supplement to the Monroe catalogue has been reprinted with the permission of the Rakow Library of the Corning Museum of Glass.

WAVE CREST WARE.
Patented October 4, 1892.

OPAL VASES, ELABORATELY DECORATED AND ARTISTICALLY MOUNTED WITH RICHLY GOLD-PLATED TRIMMINGS.

These cuts about one-third
of original size.

Vase 216—N W.	Vase 278—R Y.	Vase 217—O W.
Assortment 4, list each, . . . $ 8 50	Assortment 4, list each, . . . $14 00	Assortment 4, list each, . . . $ 8 50
Assortment 6, list each, . . . 12 00	Assortment 6, list each, . . . 24 00	Assortment 6, list each, . . . 12 00

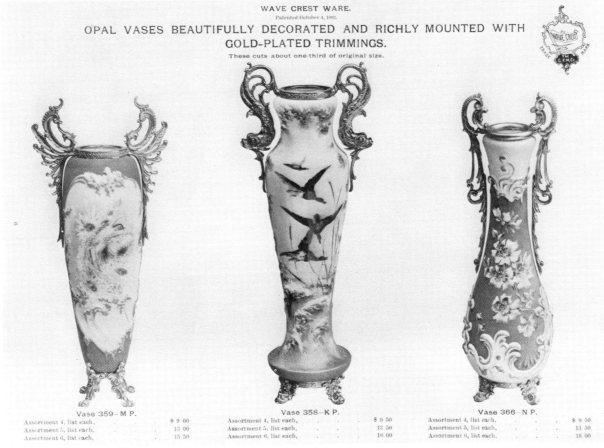

WAVE CREST WARE.
Patented October 4, 1892.

OPAL VASES BEAUTIFULLY DECORATED AND RICHLY MOUNTED WITH GOLD-PLATED TRIMMINGS.

These cuts about one-third of original size.

Vase 359—M P.	Vase 358—K P.	Vase 366—N P.
Assortment 4, list each, . . . $ 9 00	Assortment 4, list each, . . . $ 9 50	Assortment 4, list each, . . . $ 9 50
Assortment 5, list each, . . . 13 00	Assortment 5, list each, . . . 13 50	Assortment 5, list each, . . . 13 50
Assortment 6, list each, . . . 15 50	Assortment 6, list each, . . . 16 00	Assortment 6, list each, . . . 16 00

From the 1901 supplement.

The 1901 supplement to the Monroe catalogue has been reprinted with the permission of the Rakow Library of the Corning Museum of Glass.

WAVE CREST WARE.

Patented October 4, 1892.

OPAL VASES, ARTISTICALLY MOUNTED AND DECORATED.

For description of Assortments, see Catalogue 6, page 1.

Vase 353—E P.

Assortment 4, list each,	. . . .	$1 50
Assortment 5, list each.	. . . .	2 50

Bud Vase 174—1 P.

Assortment 4, list each,	. . . .	$1 75

Above cuts reduced about one-half.

Vase 365—L P.

Assortment 4, list each,	. . . .	$ 9 00
Assortment 5, list each,	. . . .	11 00
Assortment 6, list each,	. . . .	14 00

Vase 367—X N.

Assortment 4, list each,	. . .	$5 50
Assortment 5, list each,	. . .	7 50

Above cuts about one-third of original size.

7

From the 1901 supplement.

The 1901 supplement to the Monroe catalogue has been reprinted with the permission of the Rakow Library of the Corning Museum of Glass.

WAVE CREST WARE.

Patented October 4, 1892.

OPAL BUD VASES, NEATLY MOUNTED AND DECORATED.

For description of Assortments, see Catalogue 6, page 1.

These cuts reduced about one-half from original size.

Bud Vase 177—F P.

Assortment 4, list each,   . $1 30

Bud Vase 163—G P.

Assortment 4, list each,   . $1 30

Bud Vase 310—Z R.

Assortment 4, list each,   . $1 30

Bud Vase 156—H P.

Assortment 4, list each.   . $1 75

Bud Vase Globe—F P.

Assortment 4, list each,   . $1 30

Bud Vase 281—O P.

Assortment 4, list each,   . $2 00

8

From the 1901 supplement.

The 1901 supplement to the Monroe catalogue has been reprinted with the permission of the Rakow Library of the Corning Museum of Glass.

WAVE CREST WARE.

Patented October 4, 1892.

OPAL FERNERY, JEWEL STANDS AND TRAY.

For description of Assortments, see Catalogue 6, page 1.

These cuts reduced about one-half from original size.

Mounted with Richly Gold-Plated Trimmings. Trays Satin Lined, Scented.

Fernery 205—M W.

Assortment 4, list each . . . $3 50

Jewel Stand 207—D N.

Assortment 4, list each, . . . $2 00

Jewel Stand 323—P N.

Assortment 4, list each, . . . $2 25

Jewel Tray 237—B N.

Assortment 4, list each, . . . $2 00

9

From the 1901 supplement.

The 1901 supplement to the Monroe catalogue has been reprinted with the permission of the Rakow Library of the Corning Museum of Glass.

WAVE CREST WARE.

Patented October 4, 1892.

OPAL JEWEL OR TRINKET TRAYS, ARTIS-
TICALLY DECORATED.

For description of Assortments, see Catalogue 6, page 1.

These cuts reduced about one-half from original size.

Trimmings Gold Plated, Ornamented with Leaves and Fancy Knurls.

Jewel Tray 256—Z P.

Assortment 4, list each, . . . $5 00
Assortment 6, list each, . . . 7 00

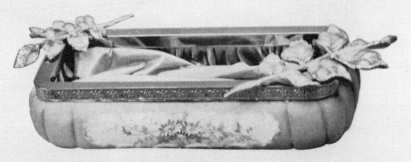

Jewel Tray 334—Y P.

Assortment 4, list each, . . . $5 00
Assortment 6, list each, . . . 7 00

Jewel Tray 280—C N.

Assortment 4, list each, ... $2 50

Jewel Tray 294—A N.

Assortment 4, list each, ... $3 50

10

From the 1901 supplement.

The 1901 supplement to the Monroe catalogue has been reprinted with the permission of the Rakow Library of the Corning Museum of Glass.

WAVE CREST WARE.

Patented October 4, 1892.

OPAL JEWEL TRAYS, ARTISTICALLY DECORATED.

For description of Assortments, see Catalogue 6, page 1.

These cuts reduced about one-half from original size.

Trimmings Gold Plated, with Figures and Fancy Knuris, Satin Lined, Scented.

Cupid Jewel Tray 288—W P.

Assortment 4, list each,	. . . .	$5 00
Assortment 6, list each,	. . . .	7 00

Cupid Jewel Tray 274—V P.

Assortment 4, list each,	. . .	$3 50
Assortment 6, list each,	. .	5 50

Cupid Jewel Tray 294—T P.

Assortment 4, list each,	. . .	$4 50
Assortment 6, list each,	. . .	6 50

Cupid Jewel Tray 142—X P.

Assortment 4, list each,	. . .	$5 00
Assortment 5, list each,	. .	6 50

11

From the 1901 supplement.

The 1901 supplement to the Monroe catalogue has been reprinted with the permission of the Rakow Library of the Corning Museum of Glass.

WAVE CREST WARE.

Patented October 4, 1892.

OPAL JEWEL TRAYS, EMBOSSED AND HAND-
SOMELY DECORATED.

For description of Assortments, see Catalogue 6, page 1.

Trimmings Gold Plated, with Ornamental Knurls, Satin Lined, Scented.

Cupid Jewel Tray 290—S P.

Assortment 4, list each,	.	$ 7 00
Assortment 6, list each,	.	10 00

Jewel Tray 264—R P.

Assortment 4, list each,	.	$ 7 50
Assortment 6, list each,	.	11 00

12

From the 1901 supplement.

The 1901 supplement to the Monroe catalogue has been reprinted with the permission of the Rakow Library of the Corning Museum of Glass.

WAVE CREST WARE.

Patented October 4, 1892.

MIRROR COMB AND BRUSH TRAY, CRYSTAL, BEAUTIFULLY ENAMELED AND COLORED.

This cut reduced about one-half from original size.

Swinging Mirror, with Gold Figure and Elaborate Gold-Plated Trimmings.

Mirror Comb and Brush Tray 354—A L.

Assortment 6, list each, ... $20 00

The body of this article and decoration is most pleasing. The effect of the satin showing through the crystal is very novel and striking, and the whole makes a beautiful article and something entirely new.

13

From the 1901 supplement.

The 1901 supplement to the Monroe catalogue has been reprinted with the permission of the Rakow Library of the Corning Museum of Glass.

WAVE CREST WARE.

Patented October 4, 1892.

OPAL RING TRAYS, AND COMB AND BRUSH TRAY, MOUNTED WITH FANCY GOLD-PLATED TRIMMINGS.

These cuts reduced about one-half from original size.

Ring Tray 363—K N.

Assortment 4, list per doz., . . . $15 00

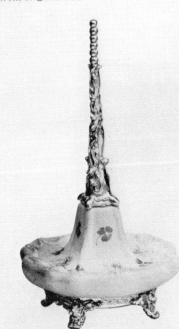

Ring Tray 363—O N.

Assortment 4, list per doz., . . . $24 00

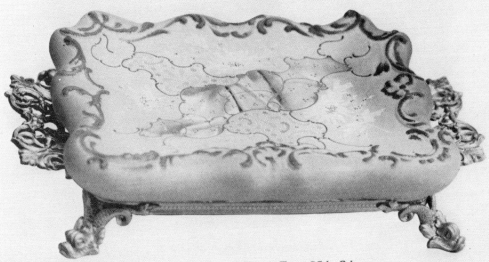

Crystal Comb and Brush Tray 354—C L.

Assortment 6, list each, ... $13 00

The body of this tray and decoration is most pleasing. The effect of the satin showing through the crystal is very novel and striking, and the whole makes a beautiful article and something entirely new.

14

From the 1901 supplement.

The 1901 supplement to the Monroe catalogue has been reprinted with the permission of the Rakow Library of the Corning Museum of Glass.

WAVE CREST WARE.

Patented October 4, 1892.

CARD RECEIVERS AND HANDKERCHIEF BOX, MOUNTED WITH RICH GOLD-PLATED TRIMMINGS.

These cuts reduced about one-half from original size.

Card Receiver 312—W N.

Assortment 4, list each, ... $3 50

Card Receiver 303—V N.

Assortment 4, list each, . . $6 50

Crystal Handkerchief Box 354—D Z.

Assortment 6, list each, ... $17 00

This style of decoration is entirely new, and the effect of the satin showing through the crystal is most pleasing, and makes a rich, beautiful and novel article.

15

From the 1901 supplement.

The 1901 supplement to the Monroe catalogue has been reprinted with the permission of the Rakow Library of the Corning Museum of Glass.

WAVE CREST WARE.

Patented October 4, 1892.

GLOVE, HANDKERCHIEF AND JEWEL BOXES. DECORATIONS IN ARTISTIC AND BEAUTIFUL EFFECTS.

Rich, Gold-Plated Trimmings.

These cuts reduced about one-half from original size.

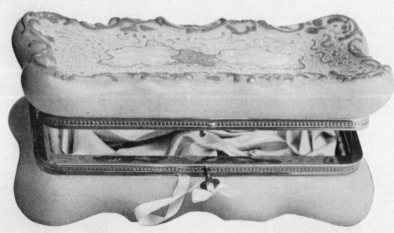

Crystal Glove Box 356—T T.

Assortment 6, list each, ... $13 50

Opal Jewel Box 373—B Y.

Assortment 4, list each, .   . $2 50

Crystal Handkerchief Box 372—B Y.

Assortment 6, list each, ... $12 00

For Description of Nos. 356 and 372, see page 15.

16

From the 1901 supplement.

WAVE CREST WARE.
Patented October 4, 1892.

OPAL INK STANDS AND HAIR RECEIVER, DEC-
ORATED AND HANDSOMELY MOUNTED.

For description of Assortments, see Catalogue 6, page 1.

These cuts reduced about one-half from original size.

Trimmings of Neat Designs and Gold Plate.

Ink Stand 361—S N.

Assortment 4, list each, ... $2 70

Ink Stand 361—T N.

Assortment 4, list each, ... $3 00
Assortment 6, list each, ...   6 50

Hair Receiver 231—S L.

Assortment 4, list per doz., .   .   . $12 50

Ink Stand 315—R N.

Assortment 4, list each, ... $3 50

17

From the 1901 supplement.

The 1901 supplement to the Monroe catalogue has been reprinted with the permission of the Rakow Library of the Corning Museum of Glass.

WAVE CREST WARE.

Patented October 4, 1892.

OPAL NOVELTIES, DAINTILY DECORATED.

For description of Assortments, see Catalogue 6, page 1.

These articles reduced about one-half from original size.

Trimmings of Gold Plate, except Whiskey Flask, that being Sterling Silver.
Appropriate gifts for Gentlemen.

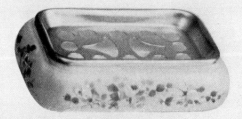

Pincushion and Tray 377—L N.			**Soap Dish 379—D L.**		
Assortment 4, list per dozen,	. . .	$20 00	Assortment 4, list per dozen,	. . .	$16 00

WHISKEY FLASK, STERLING TOP.

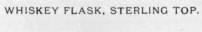

Whiskey Flask 364—F L.

Assortment 4, list each,	. . . .	$4 50
Assortment 5, list each,	. . . .	5 50
Assortment 6, list each,	. . . .	7 50

Whisk Broom 63—E L.

Assortment 1, list per dozen,	. . .	$6 70
Assortment 2½, list per dozen,	. . .	7 00

18

From the 1901 supplement.

WAVE CREST WARE.
Patented October 4, 1892.

OPAL ASH TRAYS AND MATCH HOLDER, ARTISTICALLY DECORATED AND MOUNTED.

For description of Assortments, see Catalogue 6, page 1.

These cuts reduced about one-half from original size.

Mountings of Rich Gold Plate in Artistic Designs.

Ash Tray 320—A V.

Assortment 4, list per dozen, ... $8 50

Match Holder 262—H O.

Assortment 4, list per dozen, ... $9 50

Golf Ash Tray 242—H N.

Assortment 4, list each, ... $1 50

Ash Tray 320—I N.

Assortment 4, list each, ... $1 25

Ash Tray 325—H L.

Assortment 4, list each, ... $1 00

19

From the 1901 supplement.

The 1901 supplement to the Monroe catalogue has been reprinted with the permission of the Rakow Library of the Corning Museum of Glass.

WAVE CREST WARE.

Patented October 4, 1892.

OPAL ASH TRAY NOVELTIES, ARTISTICALLY MOUNTED AND DECORATED.

For description of Assortments, see Catalogue 6, page 1.

These cuts reduced about one-half from original size.

Mountings of Rich Gold Plate of Novel Designs.

Combination Ash Tray and Match Holder.
321—B L.

Assortment 4, list each, ... $2 25

Ash Tray 171—G N.

Assortment 4, list each, ... $2 00

Ash Tray 294—F N.

Assortment 4, list each, ... $2 70

Ash Tray 294—E N.

Assortment 4, list each, ... $2 50

20

From the 1901 supplement.

The 1901 supplement to the Monroe catalogue has been reprinted with the permission of the Rakow Library of the Corning Museum of Glass.

WAVE CREST WARE.
Patented October 4, 1892.

OPAL SALTS AND PEPPERS.

Assortments 5 and 6 Traced in Gold.

AA is a Nickel Cap, single screw. EE is a Silver Plate Cap, double screw. BB is a
Silver Plate Cap, single screw. CC is a Silver Plate Cap, double Screw.

For description of Assortments, see Catalogue 6, page 1.

These cuts only illustrate our two new shapes.

For full list of Salts, see Catalogue 6, 1900.

382—A A.	382—B B.	382—E E.
Assortment 1, list per gross, . $14 00	Assortment 2½, list per dozen, . $2 50	Assortment 4, list per dozen, . $4 00
Assortment 2, list per gross, . 16 00	Assortment 4, list per dozen, . 3 00	Assortment 5, list per dozen, . 6 00
Assortment 2½, list per gross, . 19 00		Assortment 6, list per dozen, . 8 00

Boxes for Salts (to contain 2 in a Box), Satin Lined, list per dozen, $1 70

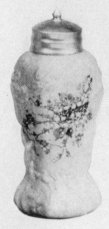  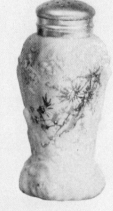

383—B B.	383—C C.	383—E E.
Assortment 2½, list per dozen, . $2 50	Assortment 4, list per dozen, . $4 00	Assortment 4, list per dozen, . $4 00
Assortment 4, list per dozen, . 3 00	Assortment 5, list per dozen, . 6 00	Assortment 5, list per dozen, . 6 00
	Assortment 6, list per dozen, . 8 00	Assortment 6, list per dozen, . 8 00

21

From the 1901 supplement.

The 1901 supplement to the Monroe catalogue has been reprinted with the permission of the Rakow Library of the Corning Museum of Glass.

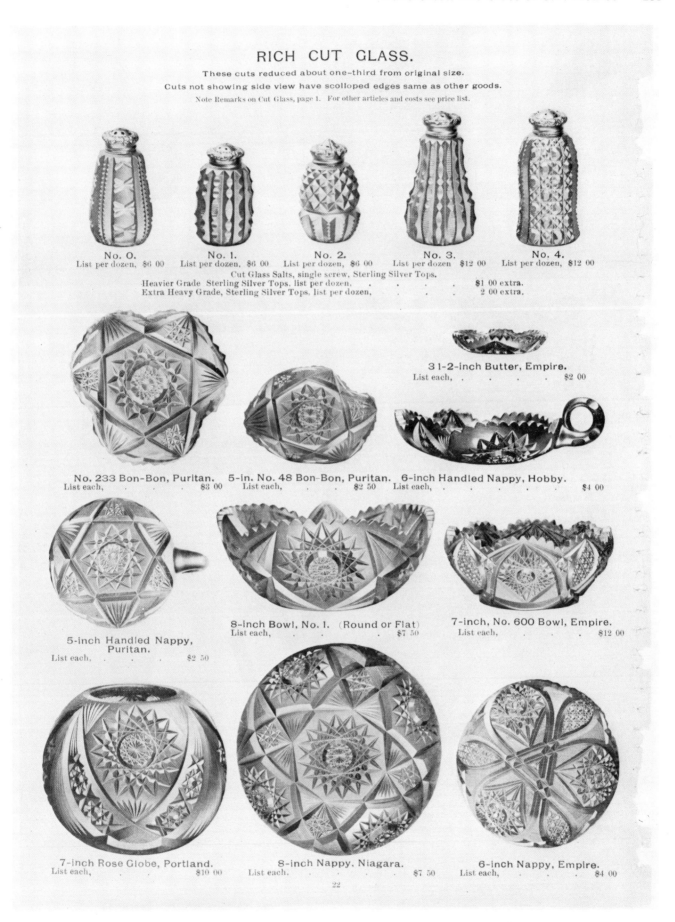

RICH CUT GLASS.

These cuts reduced about one-third from original size.

Cuts not showing side view have scolloped edges same as other goods.

Note Remarks on Cut Glass, page 1. For other articles and costs see price list.

No. 0.	No. 1.	No. 2.	No. 3.	No. 4.
List per dozen, $6 00	List per dozen, $6 00	List per dozen, $6 00	List per dozen $12 00	List per dozen, $12 00

Cut Glass Salts, single screw, Sterling Silver Tops.

Heavier Grade Sterling Silver Tops. list per dozen, . . . $1 00 extra.
Extra Heavy Grade, Sterling Silver Tops. list per dozen, . . 2 00 extra.

3 1-2-inch Butter, Empire.
List each, . . . $2 00

No. 233 Bon-Bon, Puritan.
List each, . . $3 00

5-in. No. 48 Bon-Bon, Puritan.
List each, . . $2 50

6-inch Handled Nappy, Hobby.
List each, . . . $4 00

5-inch Handled Nappy, Puritan.
List each, . . $2 50

8-inch Bowl, No. 1. (Round or Flat)
List each, . . . $7 50

7-inch, No. 600 Bowl, Empire.
List each, . . . $12 00

7-inch Rose Globe, Portland.
List each, . . . $10 00

8-inch Nappy, Niagara.
List each, . . . $7 50

6-inch Nappy, Empire.
List each, . . . $4 00

22

From the 1901 supplement.

The 1901 supplement to the Monroe catalogue has been reprinted with the permission of the Rakow Library of the Corning Museum of Glass.

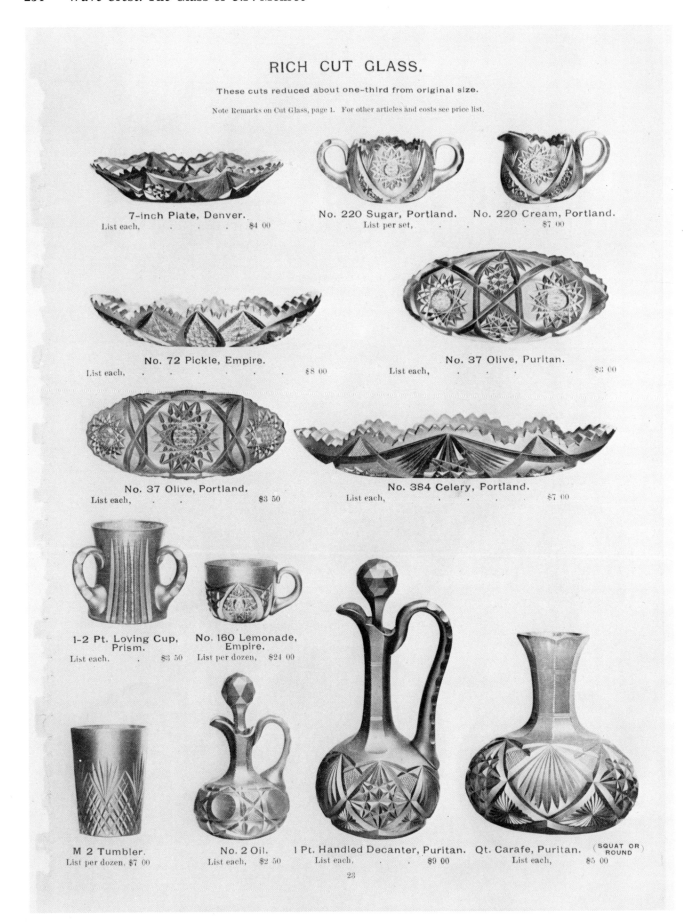

RICH CUT GLASS.

These cuts reduced about one-third from original size.

Note Remarks on Cut Glass, page 1. For other articles and costs see price list.

7-inch Plate, Denver.
List each, ... $4 00

No. 220 Sugar, Portland.
List per set,   .   .   .

No. 220 Cream, Portland.
$7 00

No. 72 Pickle, Empire.
List each, ... $8 00

No. 37 Olive, Puritan.
List each, ... $3 00

No. 37 Olive, Portland.
List each,   .   .   . $3 50

No. 384 Celery, Portland.
List each, ... $7 00

1-2 Pt. Loving Cup, Prism.
List each.   . $3 50

No. 160 Lemonade, Empire.
List per dozen, $24 00

M 2 Tumbler.
List per dozen, $7 00

No. 2 Oil.
List each, $2 50

1 Pt. Handled Decanter, Puritan.
List each,   .   . $9 00

Qt. Carafe, Puritan. (SQUAT OR ROUND)
List each,   . $5 00

23

From the 1901 supplement.

The 1901 supplement to the Monroe catalogue has been reprinted with the permission of the Rakow Library of the Corning Museum of Glass.

RICH CUT GLASS.

These cuts reduced about one-third from original size.

Note Remarks on Cut Glass, page 1. For other articles and costs see price list.

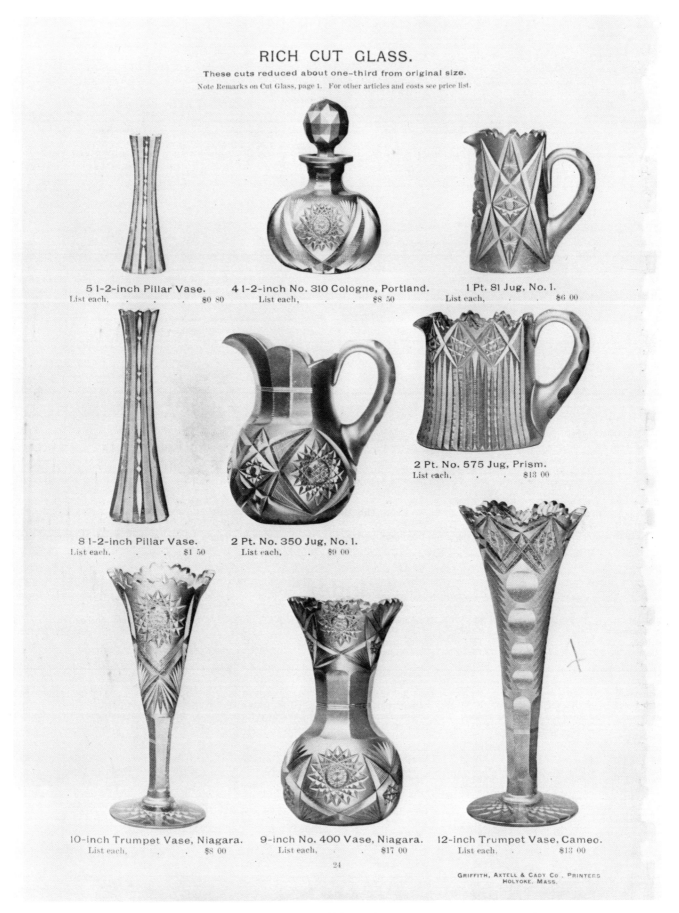

5 1-2-inch Pillar Vase.	**4 1-2-inch No. 310 Cologne, Portland.**	**1 Pt. 81 Jug, No. 1.**
List each, . . . $0 80	List each, . . . $8 50	List each, . . . $6 00

	2 Pt. No. 575 Jug, Prism.
	List each, . . . $13 00

8 1-2-inch Pillar Vase.	**2 Pt. No. 350 Jug, No. 1.**
List each, . . . $1 50	List each, . . . $9 00

10-inch Trumpet Vase, Niagara.	**9-inch No. 400 Vase, Niagara.**	**12-inch Trumpet Vase, Cameo.**
List each, . . . $8 00	List each, . . . $17 00	List each, . . . $13 00

24

GRIFFITH, AXTELL & CADY Co , PRINTERS
HOLYOKE, MASS.

From the 1901 supplement.

The 1901 supplement to the Monroe catalogue has been reprinted with the permission of the Rakow Library of the Corning Museum of Glass.

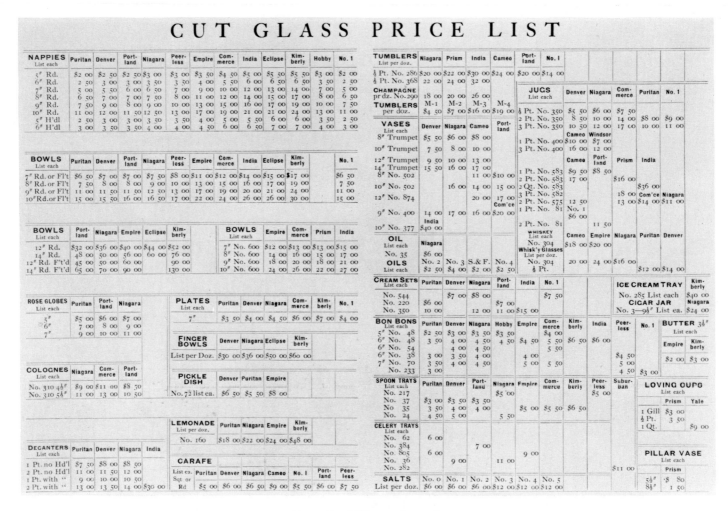

From the 1901 supplement.

The 1901 supplement to the Monroe catalogue has been reprinted with the permission of the Rakow Library of the Corning Museum of Glass.

Index

Price Guide

This price guide is done at the insistance of the publisher; the collectors and the dealers want it! The prices have been arrived at from my own experience in being involved with C.F. Monroe glass over a 15 year period. They are given in a range, and are wholly my own opinion. I have not been influenced by collectors or dealers directly, and of course they will vary with regional differences.

The prices depend on the quality of the decoration and the rarity of the piece. The rarity is my experience, and yours may differ, since no one can have a complete sampling in a country as large as ours, although, I have tried to be in most areas over the years. There is NO consideration for price differential on the basis of signatures or lack of them. The prices are for pieces that are perfect; deduct for chips, wear on the design, lost hardware etc. If a rare and beautiful piece shows up without the metal parts, it's still worth having, and possibly at only a slightly reduced price.

Please understand that prices are arbitrary. The prices given here are my own personal opinion, and do vary from region to region of the country. As in everthing, they are governed ultimately by supply and demand. Prices quoted are *RETAIL*, and dealers must buy wholesale in order to make a profit. Prices will vary as to beauty in design, and of course, rarity. The latter is important to the serious Wave Crest collector, who will pay more for a rare piece to fill in his or her collection.

ER - Extremely Rare	HTF - Hard To Find
VR - Very Rare	HP - Hand Painted
NPA - No Price Available	PR - Pair
R - Rare	SM - Small

TR - Transfer
EA - Each

Page 18
Large octagon box w/scene 1800.00-2000.00 VR
Fully cut box 500.00- 700.00 VR
Box w/winter scene 1300.00-1500.00 VR
Box w/Venetian scene 450.00- 500.00
Page 19
Box w/wheel house scene 450.00- 500.00
Box, rare aster in blown-out 500.00- 550.00 R
Box w/sailing scene 700.00- 800.00 VR
Box w/ships and water scene 700.00- 800.00 VR
Box w/ships & water scene, artist signed 700.00- 800.00 VR
Page 20
Blown-out, roses 450.00 R
Blown-out, pansy 450.00 R
Blown-out, maple leaf 450.00- 500.00 VR
Tobacco humidors 500.00-550.00 R
Blown-out, zinnia 500.00-550.00 R
Large blown out, cobalt blue 850.00- 900.00 R
Page 21
Large bon-bon 350.00- 400.00 HTF
Medium bon-bon 300.00 HTF
Covered bon-bon 550.00- 600.00 SM VR
Page 22
Medium bon-bons 350.00 EA HTF
Covered bon-bons 450.00 EA HTF
Page 23
Bon-bon w/brass lid 450.00 VR
Ferners 400.00- 450.00 EA
Page 24
Ferners 400.00- 450.00
Blank 500.00 R
Footed blank, floral panels 500.00- 550.00 HTF
Page 25
Ferneries, liners missing 300.00 EA HTF
Ferneries, footed, w/liners 450.00- 500.00 EA HTF
Page 26
Jardinieres 550.00 EA HTF
Planter 350.00- 400.00
Page 27
Large planter 650.00 VR HP
Footed jardinieres 600.00- 650.00 EA VR
Page 28
Top photo: left pair 200.00- 225.00 PR
right pair 150.00- 175.00 PR
Center photo: #1 & #2 125.00 PR
#3 & #4 100.00 PR
#5 75.00
#6 50.00- 60.00
#7 25.00
Bottom #1 & #2 125.00 PR
#3 150.00- 175.00 VR
#4 75.00
#5 & #6 200.00- 225.00 VR
Page 29
Top #1 & #2 (HP) 175.00- 200.00 PR R
#3 150.00
#4 100.00 R
#5 150.00 VR
#6 100.00 R
Center photo: #1 75.00
#2 & #3 150.00 PR
#4 60.00- 75.00
#5 & #6 150.00- 175.00 PR VR
Bottom photo: #1 & #2 250.00 PR
#3 & #4 175.00 PR VR
#5 & #6 250.00 PR VR
Page 30
Top photo #1 & #2 150.00- 175.00 PR VR
#3 & #4 200.00 PR R

#5 75.00
#6 100.00 VR
Center photo: #1 & #2 250.00 PR VR
#3 & #4 200.00- 225.00 PR R
Bottom photo: Sugar shaker 300.00- 350.00
Scroll salts, cobalt blue 300.00- 350.00 PR VR
Page 31
Stoppered cologne 350.00 VR
Atomizer 300.00- 350.00 R
Stoppered cologne 400.00 VR HP
Cigarette humidor 500.00 R
Hair receiver 450.00- 500.00 R
Cologne 400.00 VR
Page 32
Atomizer 500.00 R
Covered piece in frame 400.00 ER TR
Bottom photo: #1 650.00 VR
#2 550.00 VR
#3 500.00 R
#4 450.00- 500.00 VR
Page 33
Top photo: #1 450.00 R
#2 400.00- 450.00 R
#3 300.00 TR
#4 450.00 R
Bottom photo: #1 450.00 R
#2 550.00 ER
#3 250.00
#4 550.00 VR
#5 450.00- 500.00 R
Page 34
Top photo: #1 & #2 400.00- 450.00 EA R
#3 350.00 R
#4 & #5 400.00 450.00 EA R
Bottom photo: #1 & #4 450.00 EA R
#2 & #3 550.00 EA R
Page 35
Top photo: #1 225.00
#2 250.00
#3 225.00
#4 300.00
#5 225.00
Bottom photo: #1 250.00
#2 400.00- 450.00 R
#3 350.00
#4 275.00
Page 36
Top photo: #1,#3,#4,#6 275.00- 300.00 EA
#2,#5 225.00 EA
Bottom photo: #1 275.00
#2 450.00.
#3 350.00- 400.00
#4 350.00- 400.00
Page 37
Top photo: #1 & #4 375.00
#2 & #3 350.00- 375.00 EA
Bottom photo: Vase, blue background 800.00 VR
Page 38
Top photo: Vase, left 800.00 ER
Vase, right 1000.00 ER
Page 39
Vase, birds in flight 750.00 VR
Vase, mums on back 1200.00 VR
Bottom photo: Vase, left 600.00 R
Vase, right 750.00 R
Page 40
Vase, mermaid in sea 850.00 VR
Vase, ribbon decoration 600.00 R
Bottom photo: left and right 600.00 EA R

Page 41
Vase, "Mary had a little lamb" 1200.00 ER
Vase, rare crystal form 750.00 VR
Bottom photo: Left 800.00 R
Right 750.00 R
Page 42
Vase, ships in panel 850.00- 900.00 R
Vase, yellow roses 800.00- 850.00 R
Vase, deep rust color 900.00 R
Page 43
Top photo: Vase 850.00 R
Center photo: Vase 1000.00 R
Bottom photo: Vase 800.00 R
Page 44
Top photo: Vase 850.00 R
Center photo: Vase 1300.00-1400.00 VR
Bottom photo: Vase 800.00 R
Page 45
Vase, lady w/cherubs 1200.00-1400.00 R
Page 46
Large vase, blue 1300.00-1400.00 R
Large vase, jet black 1200.00 R
Page 47
Top photo: Vase 1200.00 R
Bottom photo: Vase 1300.00-1400.00 VR
Page 48
Vase, orchids 1600.00-1800.00 VR
Vase, pastel blue 1200.00 R
Vases, transfers of ladies 1000.00 PR VR
Page 49
Large opal box 800.00- 900.00 VR
Box, crystal, storks on lid 1500.00 ER
Medium box, crystal 1000.00-1200.00 ER
Medium box, storks on lid 700.00- 800.00 VR
Page 50
Large opal box, violet color 650.00
Large crystal box 900.00 VR
Crystal box, panel w/florals 350.00- 400.00 R
Crystal box, satin blue 700.00- 800.00 VR
Crystal box, pink color 550.00 VR
Page 51
Crystal box, Helmschmied Swirl 800.00- 900.00 ER
Crystal box, satin w/holly 550.00- 600.00 R
Crystal box, beading on top 700.00 VR
Crystal box, yellow 550.00 R
Crystal box, blue 550.00 R
Page 52
Crystal box w/beading 700.00 VR
Crystal watch box 450.00 VR
Center photo: box, left 600.00 R
box, right 700.00- 750.00 VR
Crystal glove box 900.00 ER
Page 53
Crystal vase 450.00 ER
Crystal water carafe 850.00 ER
Cigar band crystal box 900.00 ER
Non-satin crystal box, lined w/cigar bands 900.00 ER
Largest blown-out box 750.00- 800.00 HTF
Page 54
Large mirror tray 800.00- 900.00 ER
Medium mirror tray 650.00- 700.00 ER
Page 55
Mirror tray, 6" 500.00- 550.00 VR
Mirror tray, 4" 450.00 VR
Mirror tray, 5¼" 500.00- 550.00 VR
Clock box 1000.00-1200.00 VR
Easel clock 1300.00-1400.00 VR

Page 56

Easel clock, cobalt blue	1500.00-1700.00 ER
Easel clock, Ormalu fitting	1000.00-1100.00 ER
Clock box	1000.00-1200.00 VR
Covered box	350.00- 400.00

Page 57

Opal plate	500.00- 600.00 ER
Rectangular plate	500.00- 600.00 ER

Page 58

Charger, transfer	350.00 ER
Plate, hand painted	500.00 VR

Page 59

Top photo: Left	450.00 ER
#2 & #3	900.00-1000.00 PR ER
Candlesticks, blue and pink	900.00-1000.00 PR ER

Page 60

Bottom half of match box holder	NPA
Candlestick holder	750.00
Bottom photo: Decorated trays	NPA

Page 61

Top photo: Biscuit jar	400.00- 450.00 VR
Other items	225.00- 300.00 EA VR
Bottom photo: creamer, sugar & spooner	600.00 Set R
Creamer & sugar	400.00 Set R

Page 62

Top photo: Left, creamer & sugar	600.00 Set ER
Right, creamer & sugar	400.00- 450.00 Set R
Center photo: Left, creamer & sugar	400.00- 450.00 Set HTF
Right, creamer & sugar	550.00 Set R
Bottom photo: Table set	500.00- 525.00 Set VR

Page 63

Top photo: Pickle castor	450.00 ER
Early sugar shaker	350.00 R
Covered sugar	250.00
Syrup	350.00- 400.00 ER
Center photo: #1 & #4, pickle jars	450.00 EA ER
Sugar sifter	275.00 HTF
Syrup	325.00 HTF
Bottom photo: jam jar	400.00 ER
Carving set	750.00 ER

Page 64

Top photo: Set of 6 knives	125.00- 175.00 EA ER
Center Photo: Back row:	
Mustard	400.00 ER
Sugar shaker	275.00 HTF
Mustard	400.00 ER
Finger bowl	400.00- 450.00 ER
Front row: Butter pat	150.00 ER
Pin receiver	200.00- 225.00 ER
Open salt	150.00 HTF
Toothpick	150.00- 175.00
Napkin ring	375.00- 400.00 VR
Sugar shaker	275.00
Bottom photo: left, salt, pepper & mustard set	500.00- 550.00 ER
Right, salt & pepper set	250.00 ER

Page 65

Syrup	275.00- 300.00 R
Condiment set	550.00 ER
Ferner	300.00- 350.00 R
Open salt	300.00 ER
Two carafes	600.00 EA ER

Page 66

Carafe & tumbler set	1000.00 SET ER
Pitcher & 2 tumblers	1100.00-1200.00 SET ER
Pitcher	600.00- 700.00 ER

Page 67

Whisk broom holder	750.00- 800.00 R
Broom holder	750.00- 800.00 R
Spittoon	500.00 ER
Toothpick	150.00- 175.00
Syrup	275.00- 300.00 R

Page 68

Spittoon	500.00 ER
Celery Vase	275.00- 300.00 ER
Bud vase, w & w/o stopper	500.00- 600.00 VR

Page 69

Umbrella stand	1500.00 ER
Matching pr. of urns	450.00- 500.00 R

Page 70

Small brass box	400.00- 450.00 ER
Medium brass box	550.00- 600.00 ER
Clock	750.00- 850.00 ER

Page 71

Candlesticks, pastoral scene	700.00- 800.00 PR ER
China tray	200.00- 250.00 ER
Folding screen	850.00- 900.00 ER

Page 72

Lamp, "Bird on a Fence" transfer	700.00- 800.00 ER
Lamp, Wave Crest decoration	300.00- 400.00
Lamp, Nakara decoration	800.00- 900.00 ER

Page 73

Ink stand	1200.00-1400.00 ER
Footed spindle	500.00- 550.00 VR
Spindle	375.00- 425.00 VR
Ink well	1000.00-1100.00 VR
Blotter	650.00- 700.00 VR
Footed paperweight	450.00 VR
Card holder	350.00- 375.00
Paperweight	350.00- 375.00 VR

Page 74

Top photo: left, photo receiver	375.00- 425.00
center, photo receiver	350.00- 375.00
right, card holder	375.00- 400.00
Center photo: left, photo receiver	475.00- 500.00
center, photo receiver	350.00- 375.00
right, card holder	275.00- 325.00
Bottom photo: left, photo receiver	475.00- 500.00
right, match box holder	450.00 ER

Page 75

Blotters, yellow & blue	650.00- 700.00 EA VR
Whist bon-bon bell	1200.00 ER
Call bell	1100.00-1200.00 R
Napkin ring set (?)	NPA
Paperweight	450.00 VR

Page 76

Footed tray	250.00- 275.00
Footed photo receiver	475.00- 500.00
Footed ink well	1000.00-1100.00 VR
Fan-shaped photo receiver	1200.00 ER

Page 77

Humidor, Indian on horseback	550.00- 600.00 VR
Biscuit jar	550.00- 600.00 R
Cigar humidor w/lock	600.00- 650.00 HTF
Cigar humidor w/blown out shell	450.00
Small cigarette humidor	500.00 R
Large cigarette humidor w/key lock	800.00 VR

Page 78

Cigar set	550.00- 600.00 HTF
Match box	450.00 ER
Match safe	450.00- 500.00 ER
Match box holder	500.00- 550.00 ER
Paperweight	350.00- 375.00 VR
Ash receivers	200.00- 225.00 EA

Page 79

Comb, ashtray & match holder	400.00- 450.00 ER
Cigar holder, left	275.00- 300.00
Cigar holder, right	250.00- 275.00
Match holder, left	450.00 ER
Match holder, right	250.00- 275.00
Cigar humidor, left	400.00
Cigarette humidor	350.00- 400.00
Cigar humidor, right	450.00

Page 80

Smoke set, match holder & ash receiver	550.00 ER
Tobacco humidor	400.00 VR
Smoke set, metal base	400.00 VR
Tobacco humidor, w/owl	450.00 VR
Smoke set, ornate metal base	400.00- 450.00 R

Page 81

Whisk broom case	1200.00 ER
Comb & brush case	1200.00 ER

Page 82

Dresser boxes w/trays	1800.00-2000.00 EA ER
Hair receiver	275.00- 325.00 HTF
Bishop hat/biscuit jar	450.00 VR

Page 83

Pin cushion	400.00- 450.00 ER
Whiskey flask	750.00 ER
Trinket, comb & brush holder	900.00 VR
Lady's flask	300.00 VR
Footed pin tray	450.00 VR
Pin tray	300.00 R
Hair receiver	450.00 ER
Toothbrush holders	500.00- 550.00 EA R
Ring box	425.00- 450.00 ER
Open pomade	325.00- 350.00 ER
Hair receiver	275.00- 300.00 HTF
Small pomade box	375.00- 425.00 VR
Pomade box	325.00- 350.00 VR

Tooth powder box	350.00- 375.00 F

Page 84

Wave Crest boxes	175.00- 300.00 E

Page 85

Wave Crest boxes	275.00- 350.00 E

Page 86

Wave Crest boxes (center box, top photo, is VR)	300.00- 400.00 E

Page 87

Wave Crest boxes	350.00- 450.00 E

Page 88

Boxes w/cherub transfers	425.00 E
Oval box	350.00
Medium puffy box	525.00
Sq. footed box w/roses	475.00
Oval footed box, dark green	650.00

Page 89

Medium square box	525.00
Rare blank, 7½"	475.00
Footed box w/key lock	550.00- 600.00
Square box, 6½"	475.00- 500.00
Box w/maidens in woods, 6½"	475.00
Box w/maidens in woods, 5"	375.00- 400.00

Page 90

Tobacco humidor	475.00
Cigar humidor	600.00
Footed box w/florals on lid	800.00- 900.00 VF
Cigar humidor w/hand-painted maiden	1200.00 VR
Baroque shell box	650.00
Medium box, 5½"	500.00

Page 91

Large boxes, Helmschmied Swirl	625.00 EA
Box w/fish	1300.00-1400.00 VR
Sugar shaker	450.00 VF
Large box, 7"	750.00- 800.00 VR

Page 92

Box w/fish and shells	750.00
Footed box w/metal bottom	675.00
Collars and cuffs box	1000.00

Page 93

Box, rococo top and bottom	600.00
Box w/blown-out waves	850.00- 900.00 VR
Box w/mums, orchid top	700.00

Page 94

Box w/water scene	900.00
Square box w/blown-out rococo	650.00- 700.00
Box w/blue-lavendar shading	500.00
Box w/portrait	525.00

Page 95

Large egg crate box	1000.00-1100.00
Medium egg crate box	525.00
Egg crate box w/lady & beading	1400.00
Egg crate box w/petit point	1100.00-1200.00
Box in satin w/shiny motif	650.00

Page 96

Large footed box	750.00 VR
Medium footed box	575.00- 600.00 VR
Egg crate box, lt. blue w/lillies	650.00- 700.00 VR
Large footed box, gold tracery	750.00 VR
Medium footed box, gold tracery	575.00- 600.00 VR

Page 97

Glove box	650.00 R
Footed egg crate box	650.00 VR
Footed glove box	800.00- 850.00 R
Glove box w/lock, cobalt	1000.00 VR

Page 98

Glove box, pink & yellow	750.00
Footed handkerchief box	900.00
Large box w/key	950.00

Page 99

Handkerchief box w/rococo	825.00
Handkerchief box w/ver-million outline	950.00
Handkerchief box w/cherubs	900.00

Page 100

Handerchief box w/maiden on fish	1300.00-1400.00 VR
Box, cobalt blue	750.00
Medium footed box, cobalt blue	650.00- 700.00

Page 101

Footed boxes, cobalt blue	750.00- 800.00 EA
Box w/courting couple	900.00
Box w/florals	525.00- 525.00

Page 102
Item	Price
box w/heavy painting	500.00
Matched Nakara watch boxes	300.00 EA
Box w/intricate design	650.00
Footed box w/metal base	750.00

Page 103
Item	Price
Octagon box	475.00
Large Wave Crest boxes	525.00 EA
Collars and cuffs box	700.00

Page 104
Item	Price
Egg crate collars and cuffs	650.00
Biscuit jar, Helmschmied swirl	650.00

Page 105
Item	Price
Footed box w/mirror lid	NPA
Round handkerchief box	NPA
Pairpoint blank w/Wave Crest mark	NPA
Cigar humidor	NPA

Page 106
Item	Price
Various Wave Crest trays	200.00- 250.00 EA
Ash receiver	275.00
Unusual blank	275.00 R
Tray, children in sunbonnets	175.00

Page 107
Item	Price
Footed jewel trays	275.00- 300.00 EA
Large trays w/intricate designs & gold	325.00 EA
Footed tray, cobalt blue	300.00
Open trays, 7" & 5"	225.00- 250.00

Page 108
Item	Price
Ash, pin & jewel trays, 3½" to 4½"	125.00 EA
Medium open tray, russet color	250.00- 275.00 VR
Open trays, dr. green, cobalt blue & yellow	200.00 EA
Pin, ash & jewel trays, 3" to 3½"	100.00- 125.00 EA

Page 109
Item	Price
Long jewel tray	300.00- 325.00
Pin tray	125.00- 150.00 EA
Pin cushion, probable	NPA
Large fernery	400.00- 450.00

Page 110
Item	Price
Wall plaque w/maiden, 8½" x 12"	1400.00-1500.00
Wall plaque w/maiden 8" x 10½"	1300.00-1400.00

Page 111
Item	Price
Wall plaque w/lovely lady	1400.00-1500.00
Wall plaque w/winter scene	800.00- 900.00

Page 112
Item	Price
Wall plaque w/Venetian scene, dk, green	1000.00
Wall plaque w/Venentian scene, cobalt blue	1000.00

Page 113
Item	Price
Wall plaque w/floral design	1200.00-1400.00
Wall plaque w/winter scene	900.00-1000.00

Page 114
Item	Price
Wall plaque w/snow scene	1000.00-1100.00
Wall plaque w/wooded scene	900.00-1000.00
Wall plaque w/floral scene	1200.00

Page 115
Item	Price
Wall plaque, blue-grey background	1200.00
Wall plaque, blue background	850.00

Page 116
Item	Price
Wall plaque w/ferns	900.00
Wall plaque w/daisies & clover	850.00

Page 117
Item	Price
Wall plaques w/floral design, 7¼"	800.00 EA
Wall plaque w/floral design, 9¾"	850.00

Page 118
Item	Price
Wall plaque, unusual blank	800.00
Wall plaque w/pansies	800.00

Page 119
Item	Price
Wall plaque w/rural cabin	1000.00-1100.00
Wall plaque w/classic scene	1000.00-1100.00
Plaque w/floral design	900.00-1000.00

Page 120
Item	Price
Floral plaque w/roses	1200.00
Plaque w/Indian transfer	1100.00
Nakara plaque w/Queen Louise transfer	1200.00

Page 121
Item	Price
Odd-shaped plaque w/deer transfer	1000.00
Round plaque w/deer transfer	1000.00

Page 122
Item	Price
Plaque w/lion transfer	1000.00
Framed picture, painted on glass	NPA

Page 123
Item	Price
Nakara ring boxes	450.00- 500.00 EA R
Various open trays	200.00- 250.00 EA

Page 124
Item	Price
Footed bishop's hat mold box	450.00- 475.00 R
Open bon-bon tray	375.00- 400.00 R
Cigar holder	375.00 VR
Medium box, 6"	500.00
Rectangular puffy tray	350.00- 375.00 VR

Page 125
Item	Price
Ash tray	300.00 R
Hair receiver	400.00- 425.00 VR
Card holder	375.00 VR
Pin receiver	275.00 ER
Alcohol lamp	600.00- 650.00 ER
Small ash tray	250.00- 275.00 R
Pin tray	200.00- 225.00
Match holder	375.00 VR
Cracker jar	450.00- 500.00 R
Lt. pink tray	200.00- 225.00
Tray w/original lining	200.00- 225.00
Alcohol lamp	600.00- 625.00 ER

Page 126
Item	Price
Bishop's hat mold w/portrait	475.00- 500.00 R
Box w/K. Greenaway figures	475.00- 500.00 R
Footed match holder	400.00 VR
Match holder	275.00- 325.00 R
Hexagon box	350.00
"Scalloped" box mirror	375.00
Round box	300.00
Footed hexagon box	375.00

Page 127
Item	Price
Blue oval box	400.00- 450.00 VR
Box w/cherubs	525.00- 575.00
Box w/blown-out pansy	450.00- 500.00 R
Box w/blown-out iris	500.00- 550.00 ER
Boxes w/cherubs or lids	350.00- 375.00 EA

Page 128
Item	Price
Box w/cherub transfer	350.00- 375.00
Box w/sailing scenes	1100.00-1200.00 VR
Box w/K. Greenaway figures	475.00- 525.00 R
Large crown mold	750.00- 800.00 R
Box w/iris	475.00

Page 129
Item	Price
Box w/mirror in lid	550.00- 575.00
Box w/courting couple	750.00- 800.00 R
Box w/lady transfer	475.00- 525.00
Footed box, unusual shape	400.00- 425.00
"Spindrift" box	850.00- 900.00 R
Box, beaded Persian design	550.00 ER

Page 130
Item	Price
Bishop's hat	400.00- 450.00
Footed Bishop's hat w/transfer	500.00
Footed Bishop's hat, peach color	450.00
Footed box, unusual shape, peach color	400.00
Mirror box w/cross on lid	425.00- 475.00
Mirror box	425.00- 475.00
Footed box w/cross on lid	400.00- 450.00

Page 131
Item	Price
Box w/cherubs transfer	950.00-1000.00
Box w/K. Greenaway figures	750.00- 800.00
Bishop's hat blank	675.00- 725.00
Round box w/no rococo	750.00- 800.00

Page 132
Item	Price
Large bishop's hat	675.00- 725.00
Small bishop's hat	400.00- 450.00
Rectangular box	500.00- 525.00 VR
Box w/Niagra Falls transfer	700.00- 750.00
Bishop's hat mold	675.00- 725.00

Page 133
Item	Price
B.P.O.E. pin holder	275.00 ER
Open tray w/stag transfer	275.00
Match holder	300.00- 325.00
Box w/glass top & metal bottom	500.00- 550.00 ER
Hair receiver	525.00- 575.00 VR
Cigar humidor w/owl design	1000.00-1200.00 ER
Cigar humidor w/geometric design	675.00- 700.00 ER

Page 134
Item	Price
Large cigar humidor w/transfer, 7¾" x 6½"	950.00-1000.00 VR
Cigar humidor, 5½" x 4"	750.00- 800.00 R
Cigar humidor, dk. russet	650.00- 675.00
Box w/courting couple transfer	750.00- 800.00
Tobacco humidor, dk. blue	625.00- 675.00
Large box w/metal finial	775.00- 825.00 R
Cigar humidor, 5½" x 4"	625.00- 675.00

Page 135
Item	Price
Cigar humidor, blue	750.00- 775.00 R
B.P.O.E. tobacco humidor	675.00- 725.00
B.P.O.E. match holder	300.00- 325.00

Page 136
Item	Price
B.P.O.E. humidor w/unusual lid	650.00- 700.00 R
Cigar humidor w/o B.P.O.E.	575.00- 625.00 R
Tobacco humidor w/rings on side	700.00- 725.00 VR

Page 137
Item	Price
Lion humidor	725.00- 750.00 VR
Humidor, "The Old Sport", 7"	525.00- 575.00
Cigar humidor, 5¼" x 6"	700.00- 750.00
Humidor, "The Old Sport"	525.00- 575.00

Page 138
Item	Price
Match holder	300.00- 325.00
Tobacco humidor	750.00 ER
Cigar holder	475.00- 500.00 ER
Smoker's set	750.00- 800.00 ER

Page 139
Item	Price
Smoke set	750.00- 800.00 ER
Mirror tray	600.00- 650.00 VR
Vase ornament	375.00- 425.00 VR
Medium tray	250.00
Small tray	300.00- 325.00
Hair receiver	350.00- 375.00 HTF
Match holder	200.00- 225.00

Page 140
Item	Price
Match holder	275.00- 325.00
Cruet	650.00- 750.00 ER
Ash tray	250.00- 275.00 R
Mirror tray, 4"	500.00- 525.00 VR
Small mirror tray	500.00- 525.00 VR
Box w/K. Greenaway transfer	750.00- 800.00

Page 141
Item	Price
Box w/portrait transfer	1000.00-1100.00 VR
Mirror tray	500.00- 525.00 VR
Box w/ladies in garden transfer	1000.00-1100.00 VR

Page 142
Item	Price
Round box w/transfer	950.00-1000.00
Large box w/finial	850.00- 900.00
Medium box, 6"	500.00
Large box, peach w/rococo	850.00- 900.00

Page 143
Item	Price
Footed box w/goldfish	1300.00-1400.00 ER
Blown-out box, unfinished	650.00- 700.00
Pink blown-out pansy	450.00- 500.00
Queen Louise box, rare blue	850.00- 900.00 VR

Page 144
Item	Price
Footed box, rare burmese color	950.00-1000.00 VR
Bishop's hat box, hand-painted design	950.00-1000.00 VR
Bishop's hat box w/Queen Louise transfer	950.00-1000.00 VR

Page 145
Item	Price
Collars and cuffs box	850.00- 900.00
Collars and cuffs box w/Gibson girl	950.00-1000.00
Collars and cuffs w/portrait transfer	950.00-1000.00

Page 146
Item	Price
Nakara vase, burmese color	1000.00-1100.00 VR
Nakara vase, green	1000.00-1100.00 VR

Page 147
Item	Price
Vases from same blank, 8"	350.00- 425.00 EA
Small vase, hard to find shape	450.00- 475.00 R

Page 148
Item	Price
Vase, green w/pink at top	800.00- 875.00 R
Vase w/Princess Louise	850.00- 900.00 VR
Vase w/metal rim & base	750.00- 800.00 ER

Page 149
Item	Price
Planter, signed	400.00- 425.00 ER
Ferner	425.00- 450.00 R
Footed ferner	475.00- 525.00 R
Jardiniere	600.00- 625.00 R

Page 150
Item	Price
Vase, rare foot	500.00- 525.00 ER
Rare blank, handles missing	375.00- 400.00 R
Vase w/applied flowers	650.00- 675.00 ER
Bishop's hat box w/applied flowers	750.00- 800.00 VR
Round box w/Princess Louise	1500.00-1600.00
Bottom photo: left & right center	650.00- 675.00 EA VR
	450.00- 500.00 VR

Page 151
Item	Price
Box w/bisque flowers	800.00- 825.00 VR
Box w/applied china flowers	800.00- 825.00 VR

Ferner w/applied flowers	500.00- 525.00 VR	Box in blue w/pink & beading	850.00- 900.00 VR	**Page 164**	
Page 152		Oval box w/beading	475.00- 525.00 R	Kelva vases	800.00- 900.00 EA
Rare container w/Indian	450.00- 475.00 VR	Small box in blue	375.00- 400.00 HTF	**Page 165**	
Biscuit jar w/Indian	750.00 VR	Small box w/blown out rose	425.00- 475.00 R	Vase, light green	700.00- 750.00
Cigarette holder w/Indian		**Page 159**		Vase, rare dk. green	625.00- 675.00 R
transfer	425.00- 450.00 VR	Salt & pepper	300.00- 350.00 PR VR	**Page 166**	
Humidor w/Indian transfer	700.00- 725.00 R	Vase	450.00- 475.00 VR	Cut glass bowl	450.00- 500.00 VR
Salt & pepper w/Indian		Small metal box	375.00- 425.00 R	Cut glass jewel box	550.00- 600.00 VR
transfer	350.00- 375.00 ER	Medium metal box w/glass lid	450.00- 500.00 VR	Small round box	375.00- 425.00 R
Page 153		**Page 160**		Medium box	525.00- 550.00 VR
Humidor w/Indian transfer	575.00- 625.00 VR	Ferneries, fuscia & red	500.00- 550.00 EA VR	Small bishop's hat	500.00- 525.00 VR
Tobacco humidor w/Bill Cody	775.00- 800.00 R	Large box w/roses	800.00- 850.00 R	Small hexagon	375.00- 425.00 VR
Rare blotter	450.00- 475.00 ER	Oval box	400.00- 425.00	Medium box, crown mold	
Cigar humidor w/Indian	800.00-850.00 VR	Small hexagon box	375.00- 425.00	shape	600.00- 625.00 VR
Page 154		Metal box w/glass lid	375.00-425.00 R	Handkerchief box	600.00- 625.00 VR
Umbrella stand	1750.00-2000.00 ER	Rare salt & pepper	250.00- 275.00 PR ER	**Page 167**	
Page 155		**Page 161**		Mirror boxes	500.00- 550.00 EA R
Umbrella stand w/Indian	1750.00-2000.00 ER	Cigar humidor	500.00- 550.00 VR	Small crystal box, 3" x 4"	375.00- 425.00 R
Vase w/Indian, hand painted	1200.0-1300.00 ER	Unusual box w/glass lid	NPA	Small cut glass box, 3" x 4"	375.00- 425.00 R
Page 156		Cigar humidor w/cows	750.00- 800.00 ER	Cut glass bowl	500.00- 525.00 VR
Unusual Nakara price	500.00- 600.00 ER	Humidor w/"Cigars" on front	500.00- 525.00	**Page 168**	
Bon-bon, peach color	375.00- 400.00 R	Box w/pastel panels	450.00- 475.00	Handkerchief box	700.00- 750.00 VR
Page 157		Match holder & ash receiver	475.00- 500.00 VR	Bishop's hat box	600.00- 650.00 VR
Biscuit jar	800.00- 825.00 ER	Tray, crown mold	250.00- 275.00	Biscuit jar	600.00- 625.00 VR
Match holder	300.00- 500.00 HTF	Small handled tray	250.00- 275.00	Cut glass boxes	625.00- 700.00 EA V
Napkin rings	400.00- 425.00 VR	**Page 162**		**Page 169**	
Smoke set	450.00- 475.00 R	Open tray, green	225.00- 250.00	Top photo: Uncut crystal box,	
Salts	275.00- 300.00 PR VR	Ferner or planter	400.00- 425.00 HTF	left	375.00- 400.00 VR
Bottom photo: #1 & #2	550.00- 575.00 VR	Cigar humidor	550.00-575.00 R	Cut glass box, center	500.00- 525.00 VR
#3	350.00- 375.00 R	Small box	NPA	Cut glass box, right	375.00- 425.00 R
#4	425.00- 450.00 VR	Box w/gold painting	550.00- 575.00 R	Cut glass ferner	400.00- 450.00 HTF
Page 158		**Page 163**		Cut glass spindle	400.00- 500.00 VR
Medium footed crown mold		Cigar humidor	550.00- 575.00	Cut glass box, raised center	600.00- 625.00 VR
box	800.00- 850.00 VR	Whisk broom holder, blue	750.00- 800.00 R		
Crown mold box w/pastoral		Whisk broom holder, red	750.00- 800.00 R	No prices are given for pages 170-173. Pieces show	
scenes	1100.00-1200.00	Large vase, green	1000.00-1100.00 VR	are for comparison only.	

Schroeder's Antiques Price Guide

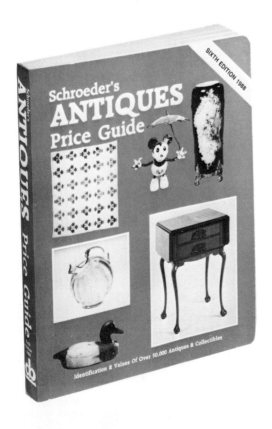

Schroeder's Antiques Price Guide has climbed its way to the top in a field already supplied with several well-established publications! The word is out, *Schroeder's Price Guide* is the best buy at any price. Over 500 categories are covered, with more than 50,000 listings. But it's not volume alone that makes Schroeder's the unique guide it is recognized to be. From ABC Plates to Zsolnay, if it merits the interest of today's collector, you'll find it in Schroeder's. Each subject is represented with histories and background information. In addition, hundreds of sharp original photos are used each year to illustrate not only the rare and the unusual, but the everyday "fun-type" collectibles as well -- not postage stamp pictures, but large close-up shots that show important details clearly.

Each edition is completely re-typeset from all new sources. We have not and will not simply change prices in each new edition. All new copy and all new illustrations make Schroeder's THE price guide on antiques and collectibles.

The writing and researching team behind this giant is proportionately large. It is backed by a staff of more than seventy of Collector Books' finest authors, as well as a board of advisors made up of well-known antique authorities and the country's top dealers, all specialists in their fields. Accurancy is their primary aim. Prices are gathered over the entire year previous to publication, from ads and personal contacts. Then each category is thoroughly checked to spot inconsistencies, listings that may not be entirely reflective of actual market dealings, and lines too vague to be of merit. Only the best of the lot remains for publication. You'll find *Schroeder's Antiques Price Guide* the one to buy for factual information and quality.

No dealer, collector or investor can afford not to own this book. It is available from your favorite bookseller or antiques dealer at the low price of $11.95. If you are unable to find this price guide in your area, it's available from Collector Books, P. O. Box 3009, Paducah, KY 42001 at $11.95 plus $1.00 for postage and handling.

8½ x 11, 608 Pages $11.95